900 years

NORWICH CATHEDRAL AND DIOCESE

a guide to the past and the present

Edited by JIM WILSON

Photo: Martin Hemmings

JARROLD PUBLISHING

Contents

ISBN 0-7117-0853-3

© Jarrold Publishing 1996

Published by Jarrold Publishing, Norwich 1996

Printed in Great Britain by Jarrold Bookprint Ltd 1996

Introduction

This book celebrates the 900th anniversary of Norwich Cathedral and of the foundation of the Diocese of Norwich.

It would be impossible to include in one book everything that could be written about the heritage of the past nine centuries, the people who shaped our cathedral, and the impact the cathedral and the diocese have on life today.

So this book is a collection of contributions all of which in different ways highlight the single theme of celebration.

It is a book for those who live in the parishes of the diocese and who are the inheritors and stewards of nine hundred years of heritage. It is also for those who come to visit our Norman cathedral, to marvel at one of the great art treasures of Europe, its carved and painted roof bosses, or to glory at our unrivalled collection of medieval parish churches.

Some contributions draw on the past. Some focus on the present. Others highlight bridges between the two. One consistent link, as we look back from the perspective of nine hundred years, is the enormous debt the county of Norfolk owes to Norwich's first bishop, Herbert de Losinga. Surely no other person has benefited our county more.

He founded our cathedral, obtaining land and endowments for it. By moving the centre of the diocese to Norwich, he established our regional capital. At a time when travel was difficult and dangerous, he united the diocese east and west by founding the county's next two most important towns and ports – King's Lynn (formerly Bishop's Lynn) and Great Yarmouth. He was influential in the foundation by Roger Bigod, Earl of Norfolk, of the great Cluniac priory at Thetford, some recompense to Thetford for the loss of its status as the centre of the East Anglian See. He set up the important Benedictine priory at Norwich. Arguably, no other institution has exercised equivalent influence on the diocese. It became a centre of teaching, scholarship, hospitality and charity, and of course worship. Its manors and estates impacted on every part of the diocese. They were a boost to the county's economy and were an important spur to improvements in agricultural techniques which in time became the region's prime source of wealth.

Jim Wilson OBE
February 1996

My grateful thanks to all the contributors to this book who have given their services freely.

The writers: Nigel Bumphrey, the late Keith Darby, Elspeth Mackinlay, Rev. Phillip McFadyen, Tom Mollard, Canon Michael Perham, Trevor Reid, Charles Roberts, Martial Rose, David Seymour, and John Timpson OBE.

The photographers: Ken Harvey, Julia Hedgecoe, Martin Hemmings, Oliver Riviere, Richard Tilbrook and Michael Trendell.

My particular thanks to Mike Fuggle who designed the book and whose expertise and advice made a major contribution to it.

I am also indebted to *Eastern Counties Newspapers Group Ltd* for permission to use photographs from their library. To the Norfolk and Norwich Records Office for giving access to documents from the Cathedral and Chapter Records, despite the problems caused by the fire in 1994 which destroyed the City Library but mercifully spared these irreplaceable historic records.

My thanks to Antony Jarrold and also to *Jarrold Publishing* for the use of photographs from their library and to their photographers Neil Jinkerson and Dennis Avon. Many others have assisted, in particular members of the Publicity and Co-ordinating Committees of Cathedral and Diocese 900.

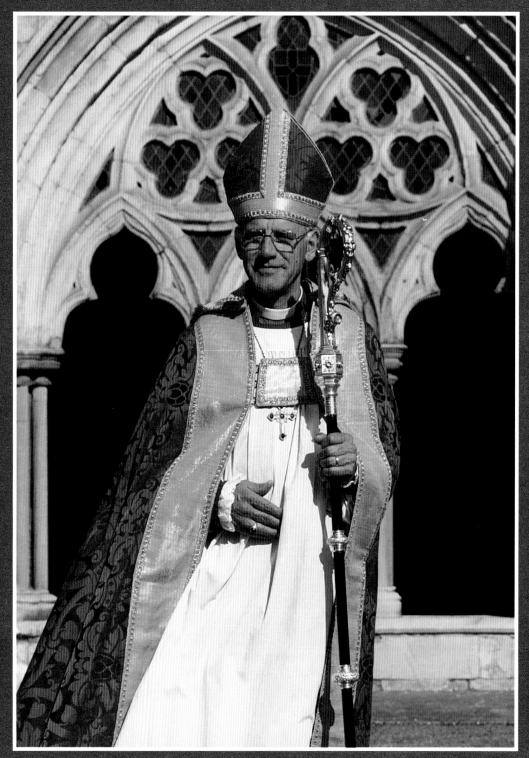

The Rt Rev Peter Nott, Bishop of Norwich   *Photograph: Oliver Riviere*

Foreword by
the Bishop of Norwich

THE RT REV PETER NOTT

WE are spending a great deal of time this year looking back over 900 years of history. That remembrance is not only good and right for its own sake, but also because it has much to teach us about the vocation of the church in our own age. The present is shaped to a considerable degree by the past, and history provides us with an essential sense of perspective. Too often we mistakenly believe that in each new age we encounter problems which have no precedent. This perspective is particularly necessary for the mission and ministry of the church, which becomes unbalanced if it does not live with a consciousness of the importance of history. The final report by the principal of a theological college about a young man on the verge of ordination noted that he had not distinguished himself in his studies but that, 'He has spent a great deal of time studying church history.' My own note appended to the report read, 'He'll be all right.' And so he will.

A diocesan bishop lives constantly with the perspective of history. One inherits, for a few years, a ministry which has continued through the centuries, and which will continue long after one is dead and forgotten. One's task is to be a good steward of that long inheritance in order to hand over the diocese in good order to one's successor, initiating change where necessary, but always in the knowledge that one is but part of a very long history.

In 1989 we initiated a diocesan strategy called 'Moving Forward'. It expressed our conviction that we should change our focus as a church in three general directions, with a new concentration on mission, with a new emphasis on shared ministry between clergy and laity, and with a new determination to shift the balance from the central to the local. That strategy has begun to take root in many places in the diocese, and an important factor in that movement has been the lessons we have been able to learn from the church's past. It is also a strategy which is intended to be long term. Not everything will be achieved in this age.

As we approach a new millennium, consciousness of the future becomes increasingly part of our present thinking. At this cross-roads in our history, it is natural to think of our life as a church in terms of movement, of a journey or pilgrimage. A pilgrim moves from the past, through the present, towards the future. The Christian faith and life is rooted in a perspective which is both historical and beyond history. Hence the pilgrimage prayer we used in preparation for this 900th anniversary as I made journeys through the diocese, following in the footsteps of my predecessors.

O Lord God
From whom we come,
In whom we are enfolded,
To whom we shall return:
Bless us in our pilgrimage through life;
With the power of the Father protecting,
With the love of Jesus indwelling,
And the light of the Spirit guiding,
until we come to our ending,
in life and love eternal.

+ Peter Norvic:

The west end of Norwich Cathedral and the Erpingham Gate to the Upper Close

From a beaver to a backhander

THE FOUNDING OF THE DIOCESE OF NORWICH

JOHN TIMPSON

ACCORDING to local legend – and I would like to believe every word of it – Norfolk's first bishop was a beaver. Many bishops, of course, have beavered away since, but this was a real one, the leader of a colony living by the Babingley River where it flows into the Wash.

In 630 AD, we are told, the Burgundian missionary St Felix sailed up the river to bring Christianity to East Anglia. Having safely navigated the perils of the North Sea, his boat got into difficulties in the river, and the beavers came to his rescue and brought him safely to the shore. The salvaged saint was so grateful that he granted the head beaver episcopal status before moving on to convert the rest of the population.

Some sceptics, I fear, may be unconvinced. Apart from the remarkable lifesaving talents of the beavers – did they pull the boat to shore with their teeth, or bat it along with their tails? – the river these days is little more than a trickle, incapable of causing problems to anything larger than a matchbox. I can only refer them to Babingley's village sign, on the main coast road between King's Lynn and Hunstanton. There stands St Felix, with his boat tossing on the waves behind him, and above his head sits a beaver on a throne, wearing a bishop's mitre and grasping a bishop's crook in its paw. It is fascinating to think that the earliest predecessor of our Bishop Peter may have been an amphibious rodent with a large flat tail, webbed hind feet, and a lifesaving certificate... .

The more serious reference books, I regret to say, discount this version of St Felix's arrival. One or two do suggest that Felix established his first church a few miles from Babingley at Shernbourne, which would indicate that he landed in that area, but the majority agree that he was welcomed to East Anglia, not by benevolent Babingley beavers but by the Saxon Sigebert, who had been converted to Christianity in France before becoming King of East Anglia, and was determined that his people should be converted too. During his years in France he had got to know Felix, and with the approval of the Archbishop of Canterbury he invited him to East Anglia to be its first bishop.

Felix did rather better than that. He became known as the Apostle of East Anglia, and he and Sigebert made such a good team that in due course Sigebert was made a saint too. They established their headquarters at a place which the Venerable Bede names as Donmoc, and the experts have long believed this to be Dunwich. In recent times, however, there has been an alternative school of thought, that it was actually Felixstowe, and certainly the name makes it sound convincing, but personally I prefer the opinion of learned folk like the late Dr M. R. James, Provost of Eton, who plumps firmly for the Dunwich theory. He dismisses the Felixstowe connection thus:

'Felixstowe was anciently called Filstow, or even I fear Filthstow; but I hasten to say that no deprecation was intended by the name. It is believed to mean a place of felled trees. The Felix part has crept in from a neighbouring priory of Walton St Felix.'

The Suffolk writer Julian Tennyson was another Dunwich supporter. 'It was a former Roman station, and very likely a large and comfortable town when Felix established his bishopric,' he wrote. 'The importance of Felix's choice must have been tremendous; churches sprang up almost overnight, and Dunwich became a kind of Canterbury, maintaining a long succession of bishops and combining religion and industry to such purpose that it stood head and shoulders above any other city in East Anglia.' No hint of any doubts there.

Alas, while pundits may contest whether Dunwich got the See, nobody disputes that eventually it got the sea – far too much of it. Over the centuries it gradually succumbed to the battering of the waves, and the last of its churches disappeared in 1919. But by then, of course, the bishopric had long since moved on. In 673 the See was divided, and while part of it continued to be based on Donmoc – identify it as you prefer – a new episcopal centre was established at Elmham. But oh dear, which Elmham?

Again we have had the experts battling it out, because there is a North Elmham in Norfolk and a South Elmham in Suffolk. Both have their ancient religious ruins, and both have their champions. Julian Tennyson, being a Suffolk man, naturally favoured South Elmham, and even R. H. Mottram, born in Norwich, gives it a sporting chance. 'This site may seem very near to Dunwich' – he is a Dunwich supporter too – 'and very ill-placed for the administration of so far-flung a diocese. On the other hand… it is difficult to avoid feeling that this was a place of some considerable importance in the dawn of East Anglian Christianity.'

But the weight of expert opinion has come down firmly in favour of North Elmham, and the most that Dr James will say to console supporters of the South Elmham claim is that the 'Old Minster', as the ruins are called, might have been first choice, but was either abandoned because of Viking raids or the bishop just changed his mind. North Elmham has now been established as the seat of the Saxon bishops in Norfolk for nearly four hundred years. Certainly English Heritage is in no doubt; it has erected signs 'To Elmham Saxon Cathedral' on all the roads around it.

Until recently it was unreservedly accepted that the ruins were the remains of the actual cathedral. Then fresh research by a County Council expert, Stephen Heywood, indicated that they only dated back to the Normans – and the Saxon cathedral had been made of timber anyway. He put forward the theory – and no one has disproved it – that Herbert de Losinga, the Norman who became first Bishop of Norwich, built a stone chapel on the cathedral site for his own use when he stayed at his palace at Elmham. He

founded the present parish church so the villagers still had their own place of worship. Because of certain similarities, Mr Heywood believes de Losinga built the 'Old Minster' at South Elmham too, as another personal chapel – and all this while he was building the great priory churches at Yarmouth and King's Lynn, not forgetting Norwich Cathedral. For the stonemasons of Norfolk it must have seemed like Christmas all the year round… .

The ruins at North Elmham

Whether the North Elmham building was a Saxon cathedral, or more likely, a Norman chapel, it was converted into a fortified manor house in the fourteenth century by a later Bishop, Henry Despenser. The extra walls caused further confusion among the archaeologists, but they have now sorted out which are which. After the Reformation it fell into disuse and was ignored for centuries, except for stones being removed for re-cycling, until the ruins were taken over by the Ministry of Works (now English Heritage) in 1948. What we can see, one might say, are the ruins of the ruins, but the Parish Council have now adopted them and they are kept in good shape.

The first Bishop of Elmham was Baedwine, an unfortunate name in view of the vineyard which has been established near the cathedral, not far perhaps from where Baedwine's monks cultivated their vines thirteen centuries ago; maybe they were not as good at it as the present incumbent. I found a list of Baedwine's successors, rather unexpectedly, in the village church at Great Ryburgh, a few miles away. There are gaps during the Danish incursions in the ninth century, but even so it is an impressive list, full of long-forgotten names like Northberht, Heathdlac, Ethelfrith and Ethelmar. There were eighteen altogether, and under their leadership churches were established all over Norfolk. The Danes destroyed most of them, but after their departure they were restored and augmented, so that by the time the Normans came there were over three hundred Saxon churches in Norfolk.

North Elmham is about as close to the geographical heart of Norfolk as you can get, and an appropriate place for a bishopric. Appropriately too, it was one of the first places visited by the present bishop on his anniversary pilgrimage round the diocese. Indeed, if it had not been for a Norman called Herfast, the Bishop of Norwich might still be the Bishop of Elmham, and North Elmham might be larger than Norwich… .

Herfast was William the Conqueror's chaplain and chancellor, and an ambitious man. He deposed the last Saxon Bishop of Elmham, Bishop Egelmar, and moved the bishopric from the rural tranquillity of North Elmham to the bright lights of Thetford, which was already a thriving commercial centre. He enlarged the Church of Great St Mary to serve as his cathedral, and Thetford looked all set to become Norfolk's premier city. The fact that William de Warrene, the king's son-in-law, was Lord of Thetford Castle, must have helped too. But the Bishopric of Thetford was only to last for twenty years, until the appointment in 1091 of the third Bishop, one Herbert de Losinga – under circumstances which were somewhat questionable, to say the least.

De Losinga came from a wealthy family in Normandy with high connections at court, but as a young man he put all that on one side and entered the Abbey of Fécamp as a novice. He must have made quite an impact – or perhaps those court connections were still useful – because he was barely into his thirties when he became Prior. In 1087 King William I was succeeded by William Rufus, and perhaps the young Prior felt it was an appropriate time to seek pastures new. It seems the court connections were still functioning, because the new king made him one of his chaplains and brought him across to England to be an Abbot.

St Felix and the 'beaver bishop'

That was the good news. The bad news was that the Abbey was at Ramsey, in the heart of the still undrained Cambridgeshire Fens, peopled by strange folk who, like the legendary Babingley bishop, were sometimes credited with webbed feet. It could hardly have been the new pasture that Herbert had in mind – more of a new bog, really – and when the bishopric at Thetford fell vacant, he decided to put in his bid – literally.

The procedure was quite common in those days under William Rufus, a mercenary-minded king who was quite happy to leave bishoprics vacant while he collected their revenues, until someone made it worth his while to dispose of them. Nineteen hundred pounds did the trick, and Herbert de Losinga became Bishop of Thetford, at the age of thirty-seven.

In simple financial terms this would have been regarded as a sound investment, but in the church it is called simony, which ranks quite high in the list of ecclesiastical sins. The new Bishop's conscience must have troubled him – or was he threatened with exposure by an eleventh-century tabloid newspaper? – because he went off to Rome to confess all. The Pope granted him absolution, on condition that he moved the bishopric to Norwich and built a cathedral there. He was also instructed as a further penance to build new churches at Great Yarmouth and King's Lynn. Thus all the major towns in Norfolk benefited from De Losinga's misdoings except Thetford, which was left with no bishop and a redundant cathedral.

This was soon occupied, however, by the great Priory of Our Lady, founded by Roger Bigod. They used it until they were able to move into their purpose-built Priory, and the town remained an important religious centre. De Losinga may have considered it a little too important for his own good, because when Roger Bigod died, leaving instructions to be buried in his Priory, the Bishop had his body forcibly removed and buried in Norwich.

That all came much later, of course. Bishop Herbert's first job on returning from Rome was to build his new cathedral, and by a happy chance – or did the Pope have it planned all along? – there was already a site for it in Norwich. The foundation stone was laid in 1096, and work began on the priory churches at Lynn and Yarmouth too. But he did not stop there. In Norwich he created five priories, founded a leper hospital to the north of the city – its chapel is now a branch library – and built the Bishop's Palace and a monastery to go with it. No doubt

he even found time to take a few services as well. He may have lacked the odd scruple, and he certainly lacked modesty – he wrote of his cathedral, 'Remember, you enjoy this advantage at my expense, whose toils and labours have won it for you' – but Herbert de Losinga got things done... .

The cathedral took nearly fifty years to complete, and he did not live to see it finished, but at the end of five years the eastern section was ready for use, and he became Bishop of Norwich rather than Thetford. There have been adjustments to the diocese in more recent times – the area of Cambridgeshire which it used to include was transferred to Ely in 1836, and a corner of West Norfolk has gone too. In 1914 the Diocese of St Edmundsbury and Ipswich was created, splitting Norfolk and Suffolk into different dioceses again, though Lowestoft and the deanery of Lothingland remained with Norfolk. But for nine hundred years the diocese has looked to Norwich for its Bishop.

There are now two suffragan Bishops, of Thetford and Lynn, but it is still one diocese, and this was emphasised when Bishop Peter made his pilgrimage, visiting every deanery and every benefice. He made a point of travelling by every modern means at his disposal, as well as on horseback and on foot: car, bicycle, motorboat, helicopter, jet fighter and hot air balloon. It would all seem as miraculous to St Felix as his rescue by the beavers does today. Happily Bishop Peter did not require their services, but if he had done – who knows?

The making of the Broads

Much of Broadland, the haunt of sailors and holidaymakers today, was created as a result of extensive peat digging for fuel during medieval times.

Norwich Priory used huge quantities of peat to burn in its kitchens. In the thirteenth and

fourteenth centuries up to 400,000 turves a year were dispatched down river to the Priory from these Broadland peat diggings. Subsequently, the man made pits became flooded and formed the distinctive Broads which are now such a unique feature of the area.

Stepping back

Herbert de Losinga set out on the road that brought him to Norwich from the Benedictine Abbey of Fécamp in Normandy where he was Abbot. It was to the Abbey of Fécamp that De Losinga's successor Bishop Peter Nott went in May 1995 to start his own pilgrimage to mark the 900th anniversary of his Diocese. In a sense it was a homecoming. The Abbey church at Fécamp, destroyed by fire and lightning soon after De Losinga's death, was rebuilt faithfully to the pattern, plan and spirit of the original, and it is easy to see where De Losinga drew his inspiration for his cathedral at Norwich.

Charles Roberts accompanied Bishop Peter to Fécamp. Writing in the Eastern Daily Press *he describes the moment Bishop Peter entered the abbey church:*

'When we walked in through the west doors and took in before us the whole vista of the building we stopped astonished – because it was so like our cathedral at Norwich.
The arches are gothic, not Norman. But all else, the flooding light, the soaring proportions, the grandeur, were instantly familiar.
"It made one realise", said Bishop Peter later, "that there was a committed relationship between this church and our cathedral. It wasn't imagination, because we all reacted in the same way".
It was from this moment that "a sense of timelessness and closeness" (Bishop Peter's words) enfolded us all. Here we were experiencing at first hand the inspiration which fired Herbert de Losinga's vision for his cathedral.'

Above right: *Fécamp Abbey. Was it the inspiration for Herbert de Losinga's Cathedral at Norwich?*

Opposite: *Bishops Hugo of Thetford, Peter of Norwich, and David of King's Lynn at the start of the 900th anniversary pilgrimage*

Photo: E.C.N. Ltd

Bishops, builders and religious conflicts

JIM WILSON

GENERATIONS of men helped turn Herbert de Losinga's vision into reality. Craftsmen, masons, and great builder-bishops all made their contributions. After nine centuries Norwich Cathedral stands largely in its original Romanesque form, a triumph to Norman architecture, to engineering and to their faith.

Down the centuries East Anglia was deeply associated with religious conflict and active dissent. More than material trade passed between the port of Norwich and the Continent. There was a flourishing trade in ideas, particularly religious ideas. Lollardy was strong in the late Middle Ages. Norwich was staunch in its Parliamentarian loyalties throughout the Civil War. And in the eighteenth and nineteenth centuries the diocese was a focus for the emergence of Methodism. These debates and conflicts had an impact on many of the bishops in whose stewardship the cathedral was placed.

When Herbert de Losinga founded Norwich Cathedral and its Benedictine Priory, towards the end of the eleventh century, Norwich was already one of England's five foremost towns.

Saxon Norwich was prominent, but it was the Conquest of 1066 which proved the decisive influence on the city.

The Norman invaders quickly stamped their dominance. Within a year or so of victory at Hastings the Normans forced Norwich's Saxon population to destroy scores of Saxon homes and to throw up the earthworks for a fortress. The first castle, completed before 1075, was built of wood. It towered threateningly over the town secure on its man-made motte. Though it lacked the permanence of stone, it was sturdily constructed and withstood siege for three months in 1075 when Ralph Guader, its first Constable, rebelled against the Conqueror. Guader was forced to flee the country, leaving his wife Emma and her force of

Bretons to hold out against the King's men.

In 1094 the seat of the East Anglian bishopric was moved from Thetford to Norwich. About the same time the foundations of the stone keep of Norwich castle were being laid, replacing the earlier timber building with a royal palace, architecturally the most important secular building of its time in western Europe.

Some Norman masons worked on both the Castle and Cathedral. Today Castle Mall has been described as the city's biggest building project since Norman times

Herbert, who had been appointed bishop at Thetford in 1091, laid out his cathedral on land acquired soon after 1086. The site of the cathedral and its accompanying priory extended to 36 acres and had been central to the Saxon town. Most of the settlement of Northwic and at least two churches were cleared and roads diverted to provide sufficient space for Herbert's great church.

Looking towards the high altar with De Losinga's tomb before it

The two massive building projects of castle and cathedral, together with the foundation of an influential priory, must have been a daunting prospect for the ordinary citizens; proof of the power and the permanence of the Norman invaders.

To create a building on the scale of Norwich Cathedral in medieval times with relatively rudimentary tools demanded daring, skill and faith.

Who planned it? Who was the designer? We shall never know, but it is feasible it was the same master mason who worked on the magnificent Abbey at Bury St. Edmunds, which was consecrated in 1095. He would have been a Norman, hand picked by Herbert and known to him, at least by reputation. He would have recruited a large work force; the skilled masons and craftsmen mainly fellow Normans; the unskilled workers English.

How many died at Norwich in the years of building has gone unrecorded but many undoubtedly perished. At Durham 200 lives were lost during construction of the cathedral there. Men fell from primitive wooden scaffolding or were crushed by falling slabs of stone or heavy beams of timber.

The master mason would have been responsible for obtaining the materials. It was probably his decision to cut facing stone in Normandy, shape it there and ship it from Caen. Local flint rubble was used to fill the core of the walls and the pillars, and woodland belonging to the ecclesiastical manor of Thorpe almost certainly provided some of the oak.

Vast amounts of materials were needed because cathedral and castle were being built at much the same time. Evidence that some of the same masons were employed at both sites is provided by identical mason's marks discovered in parts of both buildings. Given the considerable cost of shipping stone from Caen, it would certainly have made sense to import materials for both projects at the same time. Some of the stone in the two buildings is Barnack from Cambridgeshire, brought up river to Norwich after a sea trip via the Wash. In the cathedral these two stones are mixed in the early years of building, but as work progressed it is clear more Barnack stone, the cheaper material, is used, particularly west of the crossing tower.

A canal was dug from the River Wensum along what is now the Lower Close to provide direct access from the North Sea, through Yarmouth and up river. In medieval times, after construction of the cathedral and the priory, the canal remained in use providing boat access for supplies to the priory. The remains of the Norman canal were finally filled in late in the eighteenth century.

Herbert de Losinga was undoubtedly an inspirational leader. A man of strong character and driving force. Planning, fund raising and building progressed with extraordinary vigour. In 1096 work began at the east end, Herbert himself placing the first stone at the base of the Lady Chapel, near to the present-day St Saviour's Chapel altar. It was inscribed, according to 'Registrum Primum' a register of the early charters and grants made to the Cathedral Priory and compiled about 1305: 'In the name of the Father, the Son and the Holy Ghost, Amen. I Herbert the Bishop have placed this stone.'

'Registrum Primum' recalls that day, nine centuries ago: 'Then a certain Baron by name Hubert de Rye devoted to God, placing a second stone in that work, conveyed two thirds of his tithes both great and small from all his desmesnes in Norfolk. Many other great folk of the diocese gave two-thirds of their desmesnes and not a few gave one third to the monastery.'

Baron de Rye, who was Constable of Norwich Castle, was married to Agnes the widow of Herbert's immediate predecessor, Bishop William de Beaufeu, second Bishop of Thetford. Both Rye and his wife richly endowed the cathedral, as did Roger Bigod, Earl of Norfolk.

Some of the money contributed may well have been lent by Jews from a community which settled in Norwich from northern France and the Rhineland. The Jewish quarter lay between the castle and the 'French' Borough which the Normans had established close to the market place. The Jews lived there under royal protection and the Norwich community was probably second only in importance and influence to the Jews of London. Christians were not allowed to indulge in money lending, so anyone who needed to borrow significant capital had to raise it through the Jews. It is known, for instance, that funds to

Far left: *Two spiral pillars mark the point reached by the time of the Cathedral's dedication in September 1101*

Left: *Is this the ancient effigy of De Losinga or St Felix? It is open to question*

build the powerful Abbey at Bury St Edmunds came from Jewish sources, and that the Abbey was deeply in dept to the Jews of Norwich.

Herbert himself gave large sums. Numerous noblemen donated parts of all their tithes, and the citizens contributed through a tax which Herbert imposed on all dwelling houses.

The decree empowering him to enlarge the cathedral site to include a Benedictine Priory was issued by Henry I on Christmas Day 1100. It took five years for the cathedral to be completed as far as the altar sanctuary of the nave and for it to reach a stage when it was ready for use. The point is clearly marked today by the two distinctive spiral pillars. The cathedral was dedicated on September 24th 1101, to the Holy and Undivided Trinity. It took another 44 years for the nave to be completed to the west door under Herbert's successor, Bishop Eborard, and for the cathedral to reach the size it is today.

The ruthless demolition of Saxon property, the creation of two fortified enclaves around castle and cathedral, and the establishment of a privileged community of foreign monks, must have been intimidating to Norwich's native population. The cathedral and castle sites had destroyed familiar

north-south and east-west routes, forcing people to make long detours. Bitterness stirred up by this and other ownership disputes eventually led to violent conflict between the townspeople and the priory.

By the time of Herbert's death, on July 22nd 1119, the eastern end of the cathedral, its transepts, tower and four bays of the nave were complete. Also built were the bishop's palace, the priory guest house and dormitory. The refectory and other buildings had made great progress. Herbert's letters in the last years of his life tell of his impatience for the monastery to be completed. When he died he was buried before the High Altar. His monks attempted, unsuccessfully, to have him canonised as a saint.

Three early medieval paintings on the soffit of an arch of the south aisle of the cathedral have been interpreted as a reminder of the story of Herbert's penance for purchasing the office of bishop and violating the church's law of simony. The first shows him offering money to become bishop; the second him repenting; and the third building the cathedral.

An effigy in the wall of the ambulatory was long believed to represent him. It was installed in a niche above the north transept door about 1100

Looking down the nave to the great west door – the 'peoples' church

and moved to the ambulatory for protection in 1968. Whether it does portray Herbert de Losinga is doubtful. The figure, carved in Barnack stone, is certainly of a bishop holding a crozier in his left hand and with his right hand raised in blessing. It would be nice to believe this primitive figure represents the cathedral's founder, but it is more likely to be of St Felix, the missionary who converted East Anglia to Christianity in the seventh century and became East Anglia's first bishop.

After Herbert's death Eborard de Montgomery succeeded in 1121. It is possible the ancient

throne was first used in Norwich Cathedral at his enthronement. He completed the rest of the nave before he was removed in 1145, probably due to the hostility of the monks and the prior. The Norman cloisters, later destroyed in the riot of 1272, may also have been Eborard's work.

Eborard retired to Fontenay Abbey, whose foundation stone he had laid in 1139, and he died there in 1149.

The monks received permission from King Stephen to elect William de Turbe, their prior, as the new bishop.

His reign lasted from 1146 to 1174. He was the only bishop who dared to champion Becket against Henry II. In 1171 a disastrous fire, the first of several in the cathedral's long history, destroyed the craftsmanship of some of the early builders and the last three years of William de Turbe's espiscopate were dominated by re-building.

This work continued under John of Oxford, bishop 1175-1200, a noted lawyer.

Despite the passage of nine centuries most of the original Norman work remains. The great nave, the transepts, the lantern of the tower and the presbytery are substantially Norman, except for their vaulted roofs and the clerestory above the presbytery. As can be seen clearly today the cathedral was planned as two churches. The nave, without its modern seating, must have been overwhelming to ordinary people in the Middle Ages by virtue of its size and spaciousness. In the eleventh and twelfth centuries naves were the only large indoor public places and were thronged for feast day gatherings, processions and meetings as well as for worship. The nave was the 'people's' church. The choir and sanctuary formed the monk's church, reserved for their daily devotions.

For some forty years after 1200 little of importance seems to have been added. Then in the reign of Bishop Walter de Suffield (1245-57) the first great Gothic addition was built. Walter replaced the original Norman St Saviour's axial chapel with a Lady Chapel, and judging by the entrance arches which remain, it was of splendid workmanship. Sadly it was destroyed during the latter part of the sixteenth century at a time when the cathedral went through a period of neglect.

The episcopate of Roger de Skerning (1266-78) was marked by considerable unrest, culminating in the great Tombland Riot of 1272.

In a sense Norwich in the thirteenth century was a city divided within itself. The rights of the citizens and the city government had never extended to the Castle or to the Cathedral Priory. Both were islands of independent jurisdiction. The castle in the Fee of the Crown, the emblem of absolute rule. The priory under the control of the bishop and prior, second only to the Crown in its exercise of local influence and power.

Resentments smouldered over the priory's rights and its exemption from city dues and taxes.

An annual fair was held every Trinity Sunday in Tombland at which the prior by custom imposed tolls on sales. According to the 'Roll of Crown Pleas' written fourteen years after the event, the killing of a citizen, possibly more than one, by priory servants following a bitter quarrel on June 12th 1272, led to an inquest. The city coroner issued warrants for the arrest of certain of the prior's men who were suspects, declaring they should be detained 'wherever they should be,' implying arrest even within the priory precincts. The prior, William de Burnham, was furious at this attack on his jurisdiction. He excommunicated the citizens for breach of his privileges, barred the gates of the Close, and prepared to defend its walls. He is said to have sent to Yarmouth for mercenaries to help defend the priory. The trouble continued for several weeks. On August 11th some of the prior's men stationed on top of the bell tower, close to what is now the Erpingham Gate, fired on the town with crossbows and balestrae, and a raiding party from the priory pillaged the house of a prominent merchant and a local tavern.

The bishop, a former prior, did nothing to placate the mob, preferring to remain safely in his palace. His attitude inflamed matters further and the townspeople were soon out of hand. In the three days the riot raged some of the monks were slaughtered and others fled. The citizens entered the Close. Burning torches were directed at the monastery buildings and the gatehouse which were looted and set alight. The cathedral itself suffered damage. Records of the cathedral and

The view from the high altar towards the choir stalls –
in medieval times, the monks' church

the priory up to 1272 were lost in the destruction of the original Norman cloisters.

One of the last acts of Henry III before his death was to visit Norwich and preside at a thirteen day trial of citizens responsible for the damage. The arsonists were savagely dealt with. Thirty were condemned to death. Some were sentenced to be dragged through the streets behind horses until they died. Others were hanged. The city was placed under administrators. A massive fine of 3000 marks, payable over six years, was levied towards repairs. The city had to send representatives to

17

Rome to beg forgiveness from the Pope and was ordered to give a gold pyx to the cathedral. The prior did not escape punishment. He was incarcerated in the bishop's prison and resigned after the king had departed from Norwich. The city did not regain its rights from the Crown until three years later and it was a further year before the Pope's absolution of the citizens was read out on Palm Sunday 1276.

The Ethelbert Gate, largely destroyed in the riot, was rebuilt as an act of reparation, although the new building was not completed until about 1325. A room within the gateway became the chapel of St Ethelbert, replacing a church in the Close which the mob had burnt to the ground.

Repairs to the cathedral itself were finally completed under Bishop William de Middleton (1278-88) and it was consecrated on Advent Sunday 1278 in the presence of King Edward I and Queen Eleanor.

Bishop Ralph de Walpole (1289-99) repaired more of the destruction from the riot by starting the re-building of the cloisters a task not finally completed until about 1430. The slow progress was partly due to the impact of the Black Death which reached Norwich with horrific consequences in the middle of the fourteenth century. So many died during the years of the plague that Norwich lost its place as the third city in the kingdom.

John Salmon (1299-1325), a statesman-bishop, who was appointed Chancellor of England in 1320, built the great hall of the bishop's palace in 1318-25, most of which has now disappeared. In 1316 he founded the Carnery College for six priests together with a chapel, buildings which were converted in Edward VI's reign into a new home for Bishop Suffield's ancient school, now the Norwich School.

The full horror of the Black Death reached Norwich in 1349. People died in their hundreds. Half the clergy of the city fell victim. Indeed, so many clergy in the diocese died that Bishop William Bateman (1344-1355) founded a college at Cambridge, Trinity Hall, specifically to train more priests.

Bishop Thomas Percy (1356-69), brother of Henry, Earl of Northumberland, faced with typical Percy courage the fall of the timber spire in a terrible hurricane in January 1362. The collapsing spire in turn destroyed the Norman clerestory. Percy replaced the ruins with the present magnificent clerestory and a new, taller spire.

His successor, Henry Despenser (1370-1406), 'The Fighting Bishop', showed his military prowess in 1381 by donning armour and leading his troops to defeat Litester, the ringleader of the local Peasant's Revolt, at North Walsham. Despenser had gained a reputation by the ruthless way he had crushed disturbances at Peterborough where he was said to have pursued fugitives into church and slain them beside the altar. He was no less ruthless in the way he quelled the Norfolk rioters. Following the Great Schism, when two claimants to the Papacy, one in Rome and one in Avignon, split the Church, Despenser led a crusade on behalf of Urban VI against his rival Clement. After initial military success his campaign ran into difficulties. Many of his men were killed or captured and Despenser struggled home in disgrace, having totally failed to resolve the dispute dividing the Church. To this day the people of Ypres commemorate the deliverance of their city from the warrior prelate from Norwich. Despenser went on to gain further notoriety by zealous persecution of the Lollards. In 1397 a group of bishops with Despenser to the fore requested the death penalty for dissenters. This was granted after the accession of Henry IV. Despite his warlike reputation Despenser bequeathed to the cathedral one of its greatest art treasures, the magnificent Despenser reredos now in St Luke's Chapel.

During the time of Bishop John Wakering (1416-1425) the Erpingham Gate was built as a memorial to Sir Thomas Erpingham, commander of the victorious English archers at Agincourt in 1415. Nine thousand English troops under Henry V defeated sixty thousand French in one of the resounding land battles of English history. A figure of Sir Thomas is placed in a niche, showing him kneeling, his sword at his side. The word 'yenk' meaning 'think' appears on a number of small scrolls. Immortalised by Shakespeare in 'Henry V', Sir Thomas had a town house at Palace Plain opposite the bishop's palace. His tomb is in the cathedral.

Bishop Alnwick's (1426-1436) contribution to the cathedral included remodelling the west doorway and leaving funds for building the great west window. He also erected Bishop's Palace Gate.

The stewardship of Norwich's next three bishops, towards the end of the fifteenth and the beginning of the sixteenth centuries, marked the cathedral's next great building phase. They gave Norwich its awe-inspiring, lofty stone vaults. Encrusted with myriad sculptured bosses seventy feet above the floor, they portray the Bible stories from the Creation to the Last Judgement.

A disaster during the incumbency of Walter Lyhart (1446-1472) proved the initial spur. In 1463 the timber spire, the replacement built by Bishop Percy, was struck by lightning. The fire which followed destroyed the spire, the organ loft and the nave's timber roof. Lyhart decided to replace the timber roof with stone vaults covering the fourteen bays of the nave. The workmanship of the lierne vaulting, embellished by an unrivalled collection of roof bosses at each rib intersection, remains a major feature of the glory of Norwich Cathedral and one of Europe's architectural treasures. Lyhart's architect was probably Reginald Ely who had worked at King's College Chapel, Cambridge.

Ely's task was completed about 1472 the year of Lyhart's death, but the Bishop left 2200 marks to his successor, James Goldwell (1472-1499) to continue the work. Goldwell extended the stone vault to cover the presbytery, a most daring construction for its time. It rests on the thin, graceful stonework of Percy's clerestory and requires the support of spectacular exterior flying buttresses. Goldwell also re-built the spire, using brick encased in stone and raising it daringly higher than any of its predecessors. This is essentially the same spire which soars over the city today, at 315 feet (96 metres) the second highest in England.

Lyhart and Goldwell were extraordinary benefactors and they intended their names to live on. Both left their personal rebus in the form of carved puns on their names. For Lyhart a deer lying down by a stream. It appears on the choir screen and on corbels between the triforium arches. Bishop Goldwell's rebus, a gilded well,

appears on 97 of the 132 bosses studding the presbytery roof, and his chantry tomb of pure Gothic beauty is crowned by an enormous golden well. It is the only monument of its kind in England which survived the Reformation.

Richard Nykke, or Nix, became bishop in the first year of the sixteenth century and reigned for 35 years. He strongly opposed the Reformation and belonged to the old Catholic party at a time when the divine right of the Papacy was beginning to be questioned and heretical books were being distributed – the art of printing had not long been invented. Nykke strove against the circulation of heretical material flowing into his diocese from the Continent.

The cathedral's transept roofs were burnt in yet another fire in 1509. Like his predecessors, Nykke realised the best protection against further disastrous fires was to replace the remaining timber roofs with stone, completing the cathedral's magnificent high vaults, the hallmark of originality and flair with which builders of the fifteenth and sixteenth centuries enhanced the work of their Norman predecessors.

Nykke was loyal to the Pope in the face of pressure from the King. For this he was fined and imprisoned. Sadly, according to contemporary records, he died 'blind and decrepit.'

He was succeeded by William Rugg (1536-1550) who owed his appointment to his acceptance of Henry VIII's plan to appropriate the episcopal revenues of Norwich. The King substituted the income of the abbey of St Benet's. As a result St Benet's Abbey escaped dissolution, and to this day, although it is now in ruins, it is Britain's only remaining mitred abbey. Uniquely, ever since the sixteenth century successive bishops of Norwich have been able to add to their episcopal title the office of Abbott of St Benet's.

Rugg pleased Henry. In 1534, just before Nykke's death, Rugg, who had been the Prior of St Benet's, signed a statement that 'the Bishop of Rome has no authority in England'. His reward was to be appointed Bishop of Norwich.

Although Rugg had acquiesced in the dissolution of Norwich's Benedictine Priory, which took place on 15th April 1538, there was a remarkable degree of continuity between the old order and

Bishop Lyhart's rebus – a deer lying down by a stream

the new. The last Prior, William Castleton, become the first Dean. The monks became canons or minor canons. The offices of organist, precentor, sacrist, singing man and chorister were all retained and most remain today. The Statutes of the new secular cathedral even provided for the continuing use of the monastic refectory, rather like a college dining hall.

Nevertheless in dissolving the great religious foundations Henry destroyed the whole monastic system which for generations had served communities like Norwich.

The central event in Norfolk of the short reign of the young Edward VI was Kett's rebellion, which reflected the discontent of the common people with the new order. Following the dissolution of the monasteries and transfer of their lands new owners were anxious to enclose commonland and improve their revenues. The rebellion brought bloody skirmishes to Norwich where, in the summer of 1549, fighting swirled round the cathedral gates.

When Mary came to the throne it was widely known the sovereign was a convinced Papist. The year after her accession she made John Hopton bishop, a man who had been her confessor and personal chaplain. It was not a happy choice. Hopton became a bitter prosecutor of the Protestants. It was said his chancellor made wood 'dear' because so many people were burnt at the stake. In 1555 six suffered that fate, most at Lollard's Pit above Bishop's Bridge. In 1556 ten heretics

were burnt. Sixteen in 1557 and fourteen in 1558, the last year of Hopton's life. In no other diocese except London and Canterbury did so many meet their deaths in this way. But the relentless persecution only served to strengthen the growing Protestant influence in East Anglia.

On Elizabeth's accession one of the most pressing matters she had to deal with was to fill the many vacancies in the ranks of the bishops. In September 1560 she appointed John Parkhurst to Norwich. In sharp contrast to the policy of persecution pursued by his predecessor, the pendulum now swung the other way. When Parkhurst arrived in Norwich he found the diocese in a sad state of disorganisation. Many parishes were without incumbents. Parkhurst had fled to Zurich during the reign of Mary and this experience had only made him more opposed to Rome. His episcopate was distinguished by bitter and relentless persecution of the Papists and tolerance of the nonconformists.

Queen Elizabeth I visited Norwich in 1578 and worshipped in the cathedral. A magnificent throne was prepared for her opposite the tomb of her great-grandfather, Sir William Boleyn. His tomb bears the Boleyn arms which must have been a poignant reminder to the Queen of her own parents; her mother Anne Boleyn executed on the orders of her father, Henry VIII.

After Parkhurst's death a succession of men held office, but none was able to control the rising tide of religious disorder. Puritanism was growing ever stronger. Bishop Harsnet (1619-1628) attempted to oppose the Puritans but was arraigned by the citizens of Norwich before the House of Commons accused of 'tyrannous and Popish practices'. The argument went to the Lords where the bishop succeeded in providing a convincing defence. Harsnet was followed in 1629 by Francis White.

White's successor Richard Corbett, son of a Surrey gardener, was a distinctly easy going and unclerical figure and one of the most admired poets of his day. Corbett was chaplain to James I and their drinking bouts together in the royal wine cellars were the talk of the Court! He disliked the Puritan temperament but it was not in his nature to act with severity against dissenters.

In 1634 a report to Archbishop Laud found the diocese 'much out of order' and the cathedral 'in need of repair'.

In 1635 Matthew Wren, one of Laud's most loyal supporters and a rigorous disciplinarian, came to Norwich. Although he held office for scarcely two years he worked single-mindedly to establish order and conformity. As a result, next to Laud, he became the most hated of all bishops. He roused the Puritans to a dangerous pitch by repressive policies which included a twenty eight article edict, some clauses extremely controversial, through which he sought to impose order. Wren's injunctions created great bitterness. Numerous clergy were deprived of their livings for refusing to conform in matters of ceremony and ritual. In 24 months Wren's policies drove many English-born nonconformists overseas. They embarked at Great Yarmouth in their hundreds between 1637 and 1639 seeking a new life free from oppression in Holland and the New World. Three large parties set sail for New England. One included three of the Norwich master weavers, among them Francis Lawes, who took with him a servant named Samual Lincoln. Lincoln married in New England and Abraham Lincoln, president during the American Civil War, was his direct descendant.

Wren became Bishop of Ely in April 1638, continuing his anti-Puritan policies in Cromwell's immediate neighbourhood. Soon after the Long Parliament assembled Archbishop Laud was impeached for high treason and committed to the Tower. The Puritan members from East Anglia seized their opportunity and drew up articles of impeachment against Wren, accusing him of being 'Popishly and Superstitiously affected'. He was committed to the Tower without his defence even being heard, but was released after a few months and returned to Ely, only to be taken into custody again soon after the outbreak of the Civil War. He remained a prisoner in the Tower until the Restoration, almost eighteen years later.

The celebrated Richard Montagu, a writer, scholar and theologian, but no politician, agreed in 1638 to be transferred from the quieter diocese of Chichester. He died two years later before he could face a bill drafted against him by his Puritan

The exquisite chantry tomb of Bishop Goldwell

opponents in Norwich who were determined to deprive him of office.

Montagu was followed by Joseph Hall (1641-56), perhaps the most tragic of all the long line of bishop's of Norwich. Throughout his life he had shown sympathy towards the moderate Puritan point of view, but he had reservations. His writings show, for instance, he was firm in his belief in the doctrines of the Incarnation and of the Virgin Mary, so the enormity of what was to befall him at Norwich was to be all the more horrifying. Before he could take up his post he, along with eleven fellow bishops, were consigned to the Tower. They had unwisely petitioned the King saying that as they had been prevented by the mob from attending the Lords all legislation passed in their absence must be regarded as null and void. Such a claim by bishops at the height of their unpopularity was to say the least imprudent.

Hall and his brother bishops faced impeachment and were imprisoned, but not for long. He arrived in Norwich soon after Whitsun 1642. The following year Parliament issued its ordinance for the seizure of the property of all persons suspected of opposing Parliament, and Joseph Hall was listed among them. All his property was confiscated, he was evicted from the bishop's palace and humiliation and insults were heaped upon him. But worse followed. The City Puritans entered the cathedral and smashed many of its treasures. Led by two aldermen and one of the sheriffs and armed with the authority of the Government in London, they embarked upon the destruction with a will.

Bishop Hall later described the scene: 'Lord what work was here. What clattering of glasses! What beating down of walls! What tearing up of monuments, what wresting out of irons and brass from the windows and graves! What defacing of arms!'

He tells how the broken organ pipes, vestments, copes, books and other treasures were taken in a 'sacrilegious and profane' procession to the market place to be burnt on a huge bonfire. Windows in the cathedral, the work of the famed fifteenth century Norwich school of glass painting, were smashed beyond repair.

The building was left in a forlorn state and in the spring of 1644, when on Guild Day the mayor's bodyguard were accommodated there, Bishop Hall described it as 'filled with musketeers waiting for the Mayor's return, drinking and tobacconing as freely as if it had turned alehouse'.

The mayor himself was at St Peter Mancroft listening to a noted Puritan preacher deliver a sermon entitled: 'The Nail hit upon the Head and driven into the City and Cathedral Wall of Norwich.'

Bishop Hall, frail and dignified, was turned out of his palace, and later for a time the building was divided into tenements and a common alehouse.

Dr. Thomas Browne, the noted physician knighted by Charles II after the Restoration, witnessed the vandalism in the cathedral and estimated over a hundred irreplaceable brasses were ripped out to be melted down. He also described the tearing down of the tomb of the cathedral's founder which had stood for centuries before the High Altar. 'It was taken down into such a lowness as it now remains.' he wrote. The black marble slab which now marks De Losinga's tomb was installed as a replacement after the Restoration.

A musket ball firmly lodged in the north side of Bishop Goldwell's tomb can be seen today as tangible proof of these violent and unhappy events.

The desecration was bad enough, but the cathedral narrowly escaped an even worse fate. In 1650 the authorities at Great Yarmouth, no doubt at the instigation of the local MP, Miles Corbet, petitioned the Commons for permission to use lead and other materials of 'that vast and altogether useless cathedral in Norwich towards the building of a workhouse to employ our almost starved poor and repairing the piers.' Fortunately wiser judgement prevailed. When the Restoration came Corbet, who had sat on the Central Committee for Sequestration, the body responsible for the widespread desecration of churches and cathedrals, was executed.

With the declaration of the Commonwealth, the Dean and Chapter suffered sequestration and were unable to assume office again until the monarchy was restored in 1660.

During the Commonwealth years one citizen of Norwich came to the cathedral's rescue. Christopher Jay was a member of the Corporation and later served as sheriff and mayor. After the Restoration he petitioned for money from the Dean and Chapter to repay the large sums he had spent from his own pocket to save the cathedral from worse destruction. The Bishops of Lincoln and Exeter arbitrated his claim and confirmed that Jay had not only prevented demolition of part of the cathedral, but had spent considerable sums in 'needful repairs of that Church which would otherwise have fallen into very great decay if not utter ruin'. Charles II commanded Jay should be fully repaid.

The cathedral recovered its life speedily following the Restoration. The city corporation gave candlesticks which still stand on the High Altar, replacing those lost in the disturbances, and a new organ was erected on the pulpitum.

Edward Reynolds, author of the General Thanksgiving in the Book of Common Prayer, became bishop in January 1661 and for the fifteen years of his incumbency there was no further serious religious conflict. He was followed by Anthony Sparrow, who suffered sorely at the hands of the Puritans, but remained in office for nine years until 1685. In that year the country was aroused to fury again by James II's attempt to reintroduce the authority of the Papacy. Seven bishops protested and William Lloyd, who became bishop in 1685, would have added his name to the protest but his letter failed to reach London in time. Had it done so eight bishops would have appeared at the famous trial for sedition.

During the eighteenth century religious life in the diocese was uneventful, even introverted. Most bishops appointed served for relatively short periods, many as little as two or three years. Some spent little time in the diocese and cathedral life declined.

Henry Bathurst, an advocate of liberal causes, was appointed to Norwich at the beginning of the nineteenth century. He reigned for 32 years and was well regarded. Particularly high on his agenda was the pastoral care of his clergy. Bathurst voted for the emancipation of Roman Catholics, showed an unusual tolerance to dissenters, and was alone among the bishops in supporting Parliamentary reform. At the age of 87 he insisted on travelling to London to vote for the Great Reform Bill. Towards the end of his reign however he delegated many of his duties which led to some criticism. In the church at large Norwich became known, unfairly, as 'the dead See'! But his seated figure erected in his memory in the north transept indicates the affection in which he was generally held.

Edward Stanley followed, coming to Norwich with the reputation of being liberal and a reformer. He moved swiftly to deal with the scandal of pluralities and absentee clergy and was responsible for a substantial programme of building rectories in many parishes. But the cathedral was not a lively place through much of the middle years of the century. It became imbued with the 'Barchester' attitude. Holy Communion was celebrated just once a month and Saints' days were largely ignored. In 1862 an article in the 'Norwich Spectator' roundly condemned the laxity of life at the cathedral: 'Nothing can be worse than the irreverent, careless and undevotional character of worship in the parish church of the diocese'. Nevertheless, major restoration work took place under Anthony Salvin (1830-40) and Sir A. W. Blomefield (1890). Happily, the social and economic challenges brought about by the industrial revolution eventually stimulated new vigour in church life. John Thomas Pelham (1857-1893) was energetic in reinvigorating the diocese, creating rural deaneries and establishing the Diocesan Conference. It was said of him that 'his name was a byword for sweetness of character'. The Diocese of St Edmundsbury and Ipswich was created in 1914 and once again, after an interval of nearly a thousand years, Norfolk and Suffolk were in separate dioceses, although the Suffolk port of Lowestoft and the deanery of Lothingland remain within the Diocese of Norwich.

In 1930 work began building the current St Saviour's Chapel, on the site where De Losinga's original foundation stone was laid. It was the first major addition to the cathedral since the fifteenth and sixteenth centuries. In the same year the Friends of Norwich Cathedral were formed. With their support the cathedral's most sustained and comprehensive programme of maintenance has been undertaken during the last forty years.

Sir Bernard Fielden supervised work on strengthening the tower and spire in the mid-sixties, and in the seventies oak from trees donated by many Norfolk estates was used to renew the aisle roofs. A second rolling thirty year programme of maintenance began in 1994 and will safeguard the cathedral well into the twenty first century.

THE ANCIENT THRONE OF EAST ANGLIA

A rare treasure links the foundation of Norwich Cathedral with the earliest days of the Diocese. A couple of ancient carved stones, marked by fire and the elements, are among England's few legacies from early Christian worship.

The stones are all that is left of the ancient throne of the earliest bishops of Saxon East Anglia. They occupy a place of highest honour at the top of a flight of steps behind the High Altar. The stones are incorporated in a modern restoration which follows as far as practicable the original design. Medieval oak was used to construct the present wooden chair placed over the stones. Norwich is the only cathedral north of the Alps to have retained its ancient throne in its original central position.

It is virtually certain the stones were part of the Bishop's throne in North Elmham Cathedral during the eighth century. Carving on them is in the style of that period. The See of East Anglia, originally centered in 630 by St Felix on 'Donmoc', thought to be either Dunwich or Felixstowe, was divided into two in 673 and a new, largely timber cathedral was erected at North Elmham. In the eighth century it appears to have been replaced by another building and it was probably for this cathedral the throne was made. In the Danish invasion of about 870, Elmham Cathedral was burnt down and its throne smashed. The site appears to have been abandoned and neglected for nearly a hundred years until the bishopric was restored about 950 and the cathedral rebuilt.

After the Conquest it was the policy of the Normans to transfer cathedrals to important centres of population. About 1075 Bishop Herfast, who had been Chaplain to the Conqueror, transferred his cathedral to Thetford. The fragments of the throne were recovered and set up again in the place of honour. Soon the bishop was involved in a bitter struggle with his powerful neighbour the Abbot of Bury St Edmunds, who fought for independence from episcopal control and exercised his considerable influence over William to achieve it. The quarrel was taken to Rome, but both Pope and King declared in favour of Abbot Baldwin. Norwich was rising in impor-

tance and in 1094 the See was moved there away from the influence of the Abbey at Bury St Edmunds. Again the stones were moved to a place of honour in the new cathedral where they have remained ever since.

In the eighth century it was customary for the throne to form part of a semi-circle of seats round the apse. By the twelfth century this practice had given way to the throne alone being sited in the centre of the apse. Evidently, the fire at Elmham rendered one arm of the original throne unfit for use and when it was rebuilt in its present position the northern arm was replaced by the only other surviving fragment, which was an arm from one of the other seats.

Why then all this trouble to convey ruined stones from site to site and cathedral to cathedral? During the years following the Conquest it would have been particularly important for the Norman bishops to demonstrate continuity of authority with their Saxon predecessors.

But the tradition behind the Norwich throne goes back far beyond the eighth century. The first Christians were forbidden by Roman law to build their own churches, so the earliest Christian worship took place in borrowed buildings. These included Jewish synagogues, halls where Mystery cults worshipped, and basilicas or public halls. The plan of the synagogue would have included the Moses seat in a central position. Roman basilicas were furnished with a seat for the judge in the centre of the apse. Such buildings, with the addition of a Christian altar in front of the chief seat, were so suitable for Christian worship that when churches began to be built in the fourth century they were modelled on the basilican form. So it remained in Western Europe until the end of the eleventh century, at which time the builders of Norwich Cathedral adopted a very similar plan.

A shaft below the throne with a grating at the bishop's feet leads to an arch in the wall of the ambulatory behind the raised dais. This was where relics of saints were placed. The theory was the 'flue' beneath the throne enabled the Bishop sitting above to be in 'communion' with the relics below.

Care and craftsmanship

KEITH DARBY *Surveyor of the Cathedral Fabric*

CATHEDRALS have an air of permanence and of standing aside from the tide of change that has swept through the lives of ordinary mortals. Distinct changes have, however, occurred at Norwich during the last two decades, as the twin demands of increasing visitor numbers and legislation have made themselves felt. The ever-present need is to keep the fabric structurally safe, and in wind and weather tight condition, and at the same time conform, as far as is reasonably possible, with Health and Safety regulations for staff, visitors and congregations alike.

Repair techniques used today closely resemble the trades' practices of the original builders, setting aside our use of power tools for primary cutting of stone and timber. Hand tools in use today would be instantly recognised by the medieval mason, carpenter and glazier, and we are fortunate in Norfolk to have a live tradition of craftsmanship and training that ensures a ready flow of young people into these trades, who have a real interest in the buildings they serve.

Norwich has long been regarded as one of the best maintained cathedrals in this country and an example to many of our Continental counterparts. Successive Deans and Chapters through the late eighteenth and nineteenth centuries cared for the fabric, according to their lights and to the

philosophy of the age, but not without healthy controversy on occasions. In this century the Friends of the Cathedral were founded in 1930 as one of the earliest such support bodies in the country, and by far the most consistently successful. Another landmark was the revival of the medieval post of High Steward with a supporting committee of lay people devoted to the welfare of the cathedral. Access to grant aid, from the Historic Buildings Commission, for essential repairs to properties in The Close relieved pressure on the Chapter's funds and enhanced the rent roll, again releasing money for improvements not strictly falling within the remit of the Friends.

It was in 1975, after a twenty-five year stint of repairs costing some half a million pounds, that the Chapter felt able to take up the suggested rolling programme of masonry repairs around the building. The thirty year programme, initiated by Bernard Fielden as cathedral architect in 1964, had included the rebuilding of the roofs of the presbytery, nave aisles, and transepts, the stabilisation of the spire, and refacing of the south face of the tower, along with essential repairs to the other faces. The consulting architect of the postwar years, Stephen Dykes Bower, and Bernard Fielden were convinced of the value of a commitment to regular attention to masonry and glazing in particular. The programme started at the west end of the north aisle, moving eastward, with the more public signal of washing the grime from the south wall of the south transept. The same philosophy of demonstrating to the Friends where the money was being spent led from 1977 to a rather slower, but equally important programme of repairs to the cloister walls. Fortunately, the system, the Friends, and the cathedral's insurers were flexible enough to cope with gale damage to the leadwork of the north-west turret of the north transept, and with the repair of the masonry beneath, and then to switch to the west wall and finally to the east, where some very weak

This picture taken in 1959 illustrates handtools in use which and are very similar to those used by the medieval masons

Photo: E.C.N. Ltd

stonework above St Andrew's chapel roof had been revealed.

Heavy frosts during the winter of 1976 brought down a good deal of friable stonework from the presbytery parapets. Again the masons were able to switch effort to this area for a period of three years, maintaining the design of the fourteenth century work which, despite being scorched very badly in the disastrous fire of 1463, had lasted some six hundred years.

While the masons were busy outside, electricians, lighting and sound engineers were hard at work internally installing a new lighting scheme in the nave, which emphasised the three-dimensional qualities of the fifteenth century vaults and bosses while giving adequate standards for the congregation. A speech reinforcement system was started in the nave and extended in later years to the transepts and presbytery. It was supplemented for the hard of hearing by an audio loop system. During 1976 the east end heating system had to be repaired, with a hint that more work to the boilers might have to follow. It duly did, two years later.

1977 and 1978 were years of considerable staff changes. Bernard Fielden went to Rome to become the Director of the International Centre for Conservation and had to relinquish his posts elsewhere. David Mawson succeeded him as cathedral architect. In the meantime the rolling programme continued, together with a long-running campaign of overhaul of the organ.

During the early 1980's the rolling programme continued around the east end and along the south presbytery and south transept.

The disastrous fire at York Minster prompted renewed interest in our own fire precautions. Plans were made in 1984 to extend the dry riser system to ground level to assist the brigade in getting water up to roof level and to charge the sprinkler system in the spire. An automatic fire detection and alarm system, using radio links to avoid fixing conventional hard wiring to historic masonry, has proved its value on several occasions. Proposals were extended in the following years to sub-divide the nave roof space to limit fire spread, and additional first-aid hose-reels and hand appliances were provided for use by the

Sacrist's staff in an emergency before the arrival of the fire brigade. Other security measures included division of the interior of the cathedral into zones for an intruder alarm system.

1986 saw our first cathedral camp with young people from the UK and from overseas working on a variety of tasks in and around the building. The tradition has continued with only one break ever since. It was at this time that proposals for a storage, works and staff area in the angle of the north transept and the north nave began to take shape.

Shortly afterwards we were able to conserve the columns in the cloister car park – remnants of

Part of one of John Adey Repton's architectural drawings made in 1806 of the tower and spire showing the windlass used to haul construction materials to the base of the spire

Work in progress on the tower during the 1994-5 repair programme

Severely cracked north-east pinnacle

Badly eroded circular openings in the west face of the tower

the Priory infirmary. They are scheduled as ancient monuments and qualified for grant aid. At the same time the masons and conservators were working on the south wall of the library, overlooking the garden which now occupies the site of the monk's refectory. In fact the inside face of the south library wall is the outside of the north wall of the refectory, which must have been a splendid edifice. It had an upper gallery with a wall passage on both sides, similar to the cathedral clerestory, with staircases in the corners and an elevated balcony from which 'improving' chapters were read at mealtimes. On the far side of the nave the archaeologists were busy on the site of the 'Allisonium' – as the store had been christened, after George Allison the sacrist at that time. They uncovered various Saxon and early Norman burials. Similar finds had occurred when the boiler house chimney for Norwich School was built some years before. A number of drain runs and evidence of a mason's yard, with its attendant stone chippings, were found but nothing of the Saxon church thought to have been in the vicinity.

Work which began the year before on the presbytery walling and flying buttresses, continued through 1988. One of the buttresses had developed a significant bulge on each side. After suitable propping, the capping stones were lifted to reveal a hard brick core inside, largely independent of the thin outer stone casings; not at all what was expected. The claddings were re-erected with stainless steel ties and cramps.

In the following year attention was given to improving wheelchair access to the south transept, the cloisters and the west end. Among these practical measures the worshipping life of the cathedral was not neglected. St Catherine's Chapel was created for private prayer in the former clergy vestry. The nave altar was re-located further west, which gave an additional public route across the front of the pulpitum and increased communion rails for the nave eucharist. Later, the St Barnabus room, off the south nave aisle, was set aside for counselling, and the chantry of Prior Bozoun was re-furbished with a group of splendid enamels as its focal point. Work continued in the cloisters, concentrating largely on vault repairs and the refurbishing of the east, and later the south walk foliate and figurative bosses. Further work of a strictly conservation nature is awaited in the two remaining walks.

Away from the cathedral itself, a major programme of repair and conservation was under way on the Erpingham Gate. As a scheduled ancient monument, this too qualified for grant aid. Otherwise all the works described so far were paid for by Chapter funds, with very large sums donated by the Friends of the Cathedral, without whose willing and dogged persistence the building would be colder, darker, markedly dilapidated and far from the light and welcoming place we know today.

By 1990 the long forecast Cathedral Fabric Commission for England was in being. Michael Reardon was appointed consultant architect, the rolling programme and the Erpingham Gate were completed. A Fabric Advisory Committee was set up with the late Professor Andrew Martindale as chairman, and Keith Darby succeeded David Mawson as Cathedral architect, having worked on the building since 1975.

The Very Rev. Stephen Platten by the West window recently restored to its original splendour

Photo: E.C.N. Ltd

The establishment of the Cathedral Grants scheme by English Heritage in 1991/2 coincided with the next quinquennial inspection, and with a fall of stone from the east face of the crossing tower. An inspection of the east, north and west faces from a long cradle revealed further cracking in the roundel stage and behind the corner turret pilasters. After careful deliberation, the Chapter, supported by the joint Council of Friends and High Steward's Committee, decided to make an application for grant aid from English Heritage, extending initially over three annual programmes with further works to the nave, west front window, Ethelbert Gate and, eventually, the north transept north wall. At a later stage work in the cloisters was also to be included.

On receipt of an initial grant from English Heritage, scaffolding was erected in 1993 on the east face of the tower and around the lower part of the spire. This enabled detailed examination of the original construction and of former repairs, along with measurement for record drawings. As an aid to the latter, photogrammetric surveys were carried out on the north and west faces of the tower, the north transept, and the west front of the nave, with rectified photography of the glass of the west window.

The spire buttresses still carried large areas of earlier rendered repairs. Three had significant cracks. Detailed examination and drilling into the core revealed considerable areas of loose rubble, and it was agreed these should be partially dismantled back to solid material and rebuilt with new stone faces. The spire was known, from previous repair programmes, to have a brick inner structural core, with a stone weather skin bonded to it. Prior to the repairs in the 1960's these two skins had parted company and were stabilised by iron bolts and tie plates inserted at various times in the eighteenth and nineteenth centuries. Bernard Fielden's repairs eliminated these by stiffening the joints between the eight faces with stitches and a network of stainless steel wires embedded into joints of the stone cladding. Loops around the stitches enabled regular inspections to be made from the timber platforms and ladders inside, thereby giving early warning of any movement. The interior was also lime washed to make any future cracking more apparent.

What was not known was whether the stiffening buttresses around the base of the spire had brick cores, as part of the main structure, or whether they were entirely independent with just the external cladding bonded into the adjoining ashlars. It soon became apparent this was the case and that the brickwork revealed in our drillings was part of an earlier repair programme. Further examination of Dean and Chapter archives held in the Norfolk Record Office may help to pinpoint the date of this work, but this research has been hampered by the fire at the City library where the records were housed.

The north-east pinnacle was severely cracked through its bed joints and rocked when touched. An iron armature, similar to one found previously in the south-east pinnacle, had rusted and dislocated the stonework by a process known as rust-jacking, caused by expansion of the rusting iron. The pinnacle has now been rebuilt with stainless steel ties securing the original stonework.

The majority of the work on the east face itself concentrated on renewal of poor stonework in the large circular openings – five glazed to give light into the upper part of the belfry, and five infilled with stone blocks. Some of the latter were found to be sections of half-round columns salvaged in the nineteenth century from the pilaster repairs to the corner turrets. The roundels have three rings of stone 'voussoirs', the middle ring projecting in front of the inner and outer rings. Three of these had cracked for much of their circumference and were relying on little more than friction to stay in place. Judging from the very fine joints and the presence of iron packing pieces in the joints, these were nineteenth century renewals of the original Norman work which has noticeably wider joints and used oyster shell for packing to prevent the soft lime mortar squeezing out before it had developed its final strength. Modern technology, and a dearth of oyster shells, decreed the use of plastic packers in our current repairs. Cracks in the Caen stone used in nineteenth century repairs were concealed by an accumulation of soot and by the conversion of some of the surface limestone into a gypsum crust from sulphur fumes from the chimneys of nineteenth century Norwich and gasworks on the site in Bishopsgate, now occupied by court buildings. The resultant blistering is a common feature found in all the repair works around the rest of the building. In some areas late nineteenth century repointing was, we discovered, coloured with foundry ash to match the soot-laden stonework. While the latter responded to light water spray cleaning, the pointing was deeply embedded in the joints and permanently dyed. The first two bays on the north nave aisle, closest to Norwich School gates, shows this to this day.

The tower corner turrets gave us several problems. Nineteenth century repairs had cut off the original eroded outer parts of the Caen stone pilaster 'drums' and the intervening flat sections, and had replaced them with long half-round sections of stone from the Bath area, with very slim panels between them. This 'veneer' contained few 'through' stones to help bond it to the building behind, and only a scattering of lead ties to hold adjoining stones together. Instead of the myriad quite fat joints of the original construction, the new work had far fewer, thinner joints to absorb significant movement of the stonework in heating and cooling cycles. As a result the vertical joints had opened up as the stone expanded. Being unable to push up the weight of the turret top stage and pinnacle, they had moved outwards. Subsequent repairs had added non-ferrous rods drilled at an angle into the core, but the movement had continued and the cracks had enlarged. As a further precaution extra long bars were embedded deeply into the core and four full courses of through stones cut into it with larger joints to contain the overall thermal movement.

One of the problems, which has proved to be more expensive than first estimated, concerns the cast iron louvres in the belfry. These replaced earlier timber slats in the 1850's. There are records of two groups being ordered from local foundries. Over the years a combination of rust-jacking and wastage has led to a number of breakages. Given the access now available, it is hoped to extend the programme to include the necessary repairs and renewals, with improved means of fixing and access to facilitate future maintenance.

At the time of writing, the scaffolding is in place on the north face, and is being erected on the west face. The latter shows how heavily eroded the east face must have been before nineteenth century renewals. Over the years the whole of the middle ring has fallen from each of the roundels and there has been considerable loss elsewhere since scaffolding was last erected in the 1960's. Using photogrammetric drawings as a basis, we will be preparing details for the masons to make the necessary repairs on a programme agreed with English Heritage.

Elsewhere the masons have been busy repointing open joints in the stonework above and around the nave west window. Records show a long succession of alterations and repairs following reports of stone erosion and structural instability. The window itself was designed by George Hedgeland and installed in 1854. It is notable as being in the mode of early nineteenth century easel painting whereby the mullions cut across the design in each of the six main figurative panels combined with an 'antique' glass technique which sought to reproduce the brilliance and liveliness of medieval stained glass. It achieved this by using various metallic oxides to colour the glass rather than applying enamel paint to the surface of plain glass, as in most contemporary windows. Now that the glass has been examined closely both inside and out, it is clear how important the window is in art historical terms. It was taken out in 1876-78 while the stonework was renewed and refixed in position. It was probably at this stage that some of the more brilliant hues were dulled down with a layer of unfired black paint. This is now very friable and much has been lost from certain panels.

The third section of this phase of work is the conservation of the remains of the Alnwick porch containing the great west doors. This was begun by Bishop Alnwick (1425-36) who also left money for the window above. The main fabric was substantially altered and rebuilt in the nineteenth century. The porch was reduced in width by setting the outer niches in at right angles in order to allow the refacing of the nave turrets in a more truly 'Norman' design. This was probably to suit the Victorian ideal of a noble west front and in a vain attempt to rival Bury St Edmunds or Peterborough with their tall and deep porches and western towers.

It is clear from this brief account of two decades of work that the maintenance of so large and complex a building as the cathedral is a team effort. It involves a variety of professional skills, craftsmanship of a high order, forward looking policies by the Dean and Chapter, and great devotion by lay people in supplementing the cathedral's financial resources and the outside funding which has become available in recent years.

The alleged martyrdom of St William depicted on the roodscreen in Loddon church

The strange, sad – and highly questionable – story of little St William originated in Norwich in the middle of the twelfth century. The St William legend is a tragic reflection of a dark element in European history.

The Anglo Saxon Chronicle states: 'The Jews of Norwich brought a Christian child before Easter and tortured him with all the torture that our Lord was tortured with; and on Good Friday they hanged him on a cross on account of our Lord, and then buried him'.

These alleged events took place in Holy Week of 1144. According to the legend a 12 year old apprentice boy was lured away from home by someone offering him better employment. Some days later a group of men – said to be Jews – were seen in Thorpe Wood with a body tied like a sack to the back of a horse. When questioned they fled. The body of the boy was buried at the spot, but the boy's family started rumours, saying William had been seen entering a house in the Jewish quarter near to the castle. The family's allegations that the boy had been crucified and sacrificed by Jews on Good Friday in mockery of the Passion of Christ quickly gained popular currency.

Initially, Bishop Eborard de Montgomery was unimpressed by the claims. But at the Diocesan Synod meeting in Norwich after Easter the Prior of the Cluniac Priory of Lewes, who was in the county visiting a dependent Cluniac Abbey at Castle Acre, begged Eborard to allow him to take the body of the 'holy boy' back to Lewes, where the martyr's relics would attract the veneration of the faithful. Once at Lewes, he said, no amount of money would induce him to allow the body to be moved elsewhere. This persuaded many of the monks at Norwich that the boy was indeed a martyr and his body should not be taken from them. Eventually Eborard agreed the body should be exhumed and buried in the monk's cemetery within the precinct of the cathedral. A year or so later a chapel was erected at the site on Mousehold where the boy's body had first been buried. Earthworks of that building remain today.

In 1150 Thomas of Monmouth, a monk at Norwich priory, took up the cause. He said he had a dream in which he was visited by the cathedral's founder, Herbert de Losinga, which convinced him William was a saint and a martyr. He persuaded the Prior to have the little skeleton exhumed and re-interred in the Priory Chapter House where it would be more fitting for pilgrims to visit the tomb. So the cult of St William flourished,

stimulated within the priory no doubt by knowledge that the cathedral would benefit financially if it had a saint associated with it to attract pilgrims and bring trade.

If that was the motive, it certainly worked. Pilgrims began to visit the grave in such numbers their presence at the Chapter House was disrupting the work of the Priory. A more appropriate burial place became necessary and Bishop William de Turbe, who succeeded Eborard and was far more disposed to believe the crucifixion story, agreed around 1154 to the body being moved to a martyr's chapel within the cathedral, now the Jesus Chapel. An altar to St William was also installed against the north side of the choir screen. References to it appear in the cathedral records as late as the middle of the fifteenth century. Eventually the boy was 'canonised' and Thomas of Monmouth wrote a book entitled 'The Life and Miracles of St William' which recorded many 'miracles' said to have taken place around the shrine over a period of 20 years. Few other medieval cults drew so many pilgrims, particularly from the local area. His feast day was celebrated at Norwich every March 24th.

The story probably owes more to legend than to fact, but it laid the foundations of a potent belief that was to rear its head constantly through the ages. There are examples of similar stories of boy 'martyrs' murdered by Jews elsewhere in England, notably Harold of Gloucester (1168), and closer to Norwich, an incident at Bury St Edmunds in 1181. Perhaps the most famous was the 'murder' of a Christian boy called Hugh at Lincoln in 1255. It is unlikely the Norwich torture and sacrifice ever took place. If it did it is improbable William's death was at the hands of Jews whose religion would not have accepted child sacrifice. There was a strong undercurrent of dislike of the Jews their wealth and their influence in Norwich at that time, an emotion which gained currency throughout East Anglia as the William cult spread. The Jews had come over with the Normans and were under the protection of the Crown. They were seen as part of the new alien governing establishment. In Bury St Edmunds the Jewish quarter was known as Heathenman's Street and feelings there ran so high fifty-seven Jews were slaughtered on Palm Sunday 1190. The legend, whether soundly based or not, is the first recorded example of a dangerous thread of anti-Semitism which has run through history and which directly links the twelfth century to the terrible events which occurred in the holocaust of the present century.

(1) God blesses his creation (nave)

Sermons carved in wood and stone

MARTIAL ROSE

GOTHIC stone-ribbed vaulting appearing from the end of the thirteenth century required keystones to hold the ribs in place. A roof boss is a keystone on whose underside is frequently a carving. Such carvings are an attractive feature of many of our medieval churches and cathedrals. The carvings are often of a foliate or floral kind, sometimes they depict scenes from scripture or the lives of the saints, and sometimes there are Green Men, monstrous beasts and hybrids – part man part beast.

Norwich Cathedral has about a thousand roof bosses. Compared with other English Gothic cathedrals the number itself is not particularly striking. What is unique to Norwich, however, is that unlike other churches and cathedrals, the majority of the Norwich bosses are story-telling: that is, they are not only historiated-figured carvings, but form sequences, even great cycles, of stories. For instance, within the cloisters there is a cycle of 102 carvings on the theme of the Apocalypse, the Book of Revelation, and in the nave there is a cycle of more than 250 bosses on the history of the world, as understood in the Middle Ages, from the Creation to the Last Judgement. But there are great numbers of bosses that tell stories within themselves such as the north cloister boss which includes Salome dancing before Herod, St John the Baptist being beheaded, and Salome offering to Herod the Baptist's head on a dish. There are also the sequences of bosses, perhaps two or three, sometimes as many as five together telling the story of the saints such as St Clement, St Denis, St Theophilus or St Thomas.

The Cloisters   It was in the cloisters at Norwich where the roof bosses first appeared. The Norman cloisters, probably badly damaged in the riots and fire of 1272, were gradually replaced by a stone-vaulted structure, with traceried windows facing onto the garth or inner garden. The building took from the end of the thirteenth century until the middle of the fifteenth century to complete. It was clearly not seen as a high priority. The work was undertaken piecemeal when funds became available, when a competent work force with appropriate materials could be assembled, and when plague was not rampant.

There are forty-nine bays, including the four corner bays. The design of the vaulting is of a central ridge intersected by a series of transverse ribs. At each point of intersection a keystone is inserted. Apart from two exceptions, in each bay there are eight carved bosses. In all there are 394 bosses.

In the early fourteenth century when the first carvings were undertaken I doubt whether there was any overall design governing the subject matter of the bosses laid down by bishop or prior. Work began in the middle of the east walk by the Chapter House doors and reached the south end of the walk with foliage as the motif. Leaves of many kinds abound: oak, vine, hawthorn, ivy, maple, acanthus, carved exquisitely and in a realistic vein as though the sculptor was closely observing the detail of the leaf (Photo. 2).

At the south end of the east walk figured carvings appear for the first time: a dragon is seen among oak leaves eating acorns; a Green Man peers menacingly out from a mask of hawthorn leaves; a man-monster, set in a wreath of acanthus leaves, with two cowled heads stemming from one neck, without any body but with large clawed feet. Such figures might be seen in the decorated marginalia of medieval illuminated manuscripts (Photo. 3).

The next phase of carving took place in the east walk from the Chapter House doors moving northwards towards the entry to the Cathedral, the Prior's Door. In this section the carving is

(2) Foliage: (cloister, east walk)

(3) Hybrid: (cloister, east walk)

quite different in intent and execution. The main emphasis is on figured carving not merely foliage. Nevertheless the figured work is nearly always set within a wreath of foliage. The subjects are very varied: men with shield and buckler fighting dragons; the tabor and pipe players; foxes devouring fowl; the four Evangelists with their attendant symbols; and, most significantly, the first series of historiated bosses. The subject of this sequence of five is the Passion of Christ: the Flagellation; the Carrying of the Cross; the Crucifixion; the Resurrection; and the Harrowing of Hell. Not only is each of these carvings set within a wreath of leaves but the leaves themselves intrude into the central scene and play a distinct role. For instance in the Flagellation (Photo. 4) Christ appears to be bound to the trunk of a vine from which grow leaves which partly cover the tunics of the flagellators and a bunch of grapes is seen between Christ, 'the true vine', and one of his tormentors. In the Crucifixion foliage grows from the arms of the cross as though the body of Christ gives life to the dead wood.

This first sequence of five bosses is located along the south-north ridge which runs towards the Prior's Door, and each of the bosses is placed centrally within its bay. The subjects surrounding them, apart from the four Evangelists at the apex

of the wall arches, and a much damaged carving of the martyrdom of St Edmund, are entirely secular. But within most of these bosses there is much latent story material. For instance there is the wife who has caught a Puck-like creature stealing the washing from her line (Photo. 5). She is evidently enjoying the punishment she is meting out while he winces in her tight hold, still clutching a garment in each hand.

The vaulting in the east walk was being completed in the second and third decades of the fourteenth century. The south walk vaulting was in hand during the third decade, and ten of the eleven bays were completed before the Black Death in 1349 took such a heavy toll of the citizens of Norwich including monks and masons. But before the carving commenced in the south walk a master plan had been developed which was to unfold on a grand scale. Whereas the subject matter for the east walk bosses, apart from the Passion sequence, seems to have been chosen at random, the south walk begins with the first of the Apocalypse carvings. The Revelation of St John the Divine, the last book of the Bible, often called the Apocalypse, recounts the vision of St John in exile on the Island of Patmos. An angel appears to him and exhorts him to write down his vision of the Son of Man (Photo. 6), of the glories

(4) The Flagellation, (cloister, east walk)

(5) Thief caught stealing the washing – (cloister, east walk)

of heaven, and of the terrible afflictions which will assail unrepentant man. He writes of the forces of evil, the beast with seven heads, the Whore of Babylon, and lastly of the path that leads to the celestial city.

This story had been told in very many Apocalypse manuscripts, often containing about ninety illustrations. One such manuscript would have been available to the bishop and prior of Norwich before the claustral project was undertaken. Once in hand we know that there was a request in 1346, probably from the masons, for 'a history of the Apocalypse'. It would appear that the original scheme was for about one hundred carvings of the Apocalypse to be placed along the central ridge of the three walks, south, west, and north, with just over thirty bosses allotted to each walk. This is indicated by the spacing of the bosses in the south walk. However, when work was recommenced in the fifteenth century such a scheme soon gave way to a directive to complete the cycle within the west walk.

Cycles of the Apocalypse have manifested themselves in church art in different ways: the stone carvings in the voussoirs of the portals at Rheims Cathedral; the wall-paintings in the Chapter House of Westminster Abbey; the east window of York Minster; the tapestries at Anger;

(6) St John's vision of the Son of Man – (cloister, south walk)

the rose window of Ste Chapelle. There was no precedent for the mode of treatment of the subject undertaken by Norwich Priory in the early part of the fourteenth century. The carvings were based most probably on an East Anglian manuscript of the Apocalypse, and the result was a cycle of 102 bosses. Unfortunately many of the bosses have suffered from vandalism and weathering, but sufficient remains to demonstrate the imagination and courage of a great undertaking and the skill and determination which brought it to a successful conclusion.

The Apocalypse carvings can be considered in four sections: St John's vision of the Son of Man and the opening of the seven seals of the Lamb's Book of Life; the seven angels blowing the seven trumpets and the War in Heaven; the angels opening the seven vials; the destruction of Babylon, the binding of Satan, the damnation of the wicked and the receiving of the righteous into heaven. The cycle comes to its conclusion at the north end of the west walk just before the Monks' Door leading into the Cathedral. The revised design must have taken this into account. Such an entry into the Cathedral is analogous to that at the north end of the east walk whereby the monks on their way to their Offices passed beneath the bosses depicting Christ's Passion with the Evangelists looking down on them from above right, and as they passed through the Prior's Door there was Christ in Judgement, showing his wounds, flanked by angels with symbols of his Passion, and St Edmund, an East Anglian saint, Moses with the tablets of the law, St Peter holding the Church in his hand, and St John the Baptist in a hair shirt.

Thirty-nine Apocalypse bosses are in the west walk and sixty-three in the south walk. There are consequently many other carvings in these walks and they are on a wide variety of different themes. But there are relatively few on scriptural themes. These are: an Annunciation; a Visitation – of the Virgin Mary to her cousin Elizabeth; the beheading of John the Baptist (Photo. 7); Samson fighting with a lion. In the west walk there are three sequences over the wall arches. Four bosses tell the story of St Basil and Julian the Apostate, with the gracious intervention of the Virgin Mary;

three carvings tell a tale of the Christian of Constantinople, again with the intercession of the Virgin Mary; and two bosses at the north end are on the theme of St Christopher.

Some of the vaulting in the west walk was contemporary with that in the north walk where the carving of the bosses was completed in about 1430 leaving just the paving to be done which was not put in hand until 1450. The north walk contains some of the most attractive sculpture in the cloisters. It comprises the continuation of resurrection and post resurrection themes from the east end and develops into the death and coronation of the Virgin together with the death and assumption of St John the Evangelist. The lives and martyrdoms of the saints are liberally treated. Of particular interest is a series of five bosses on the martyrdom of St Thomas of Canterbury. One of these shows King Henry II, naked apart from his drawers (Photo. 8), praying at the shrine of the saint, being scourged by three monks while his courtiers stand by holding his clothes. The king's crown lies on the ground in front of him. In 1538 King Henry VIII had ordered the despoliation of the shrine of St Thomas and all images associated with the saint. King Henry would have been little pleased to have seen this survival in the Norwich cloister.

Many of the cloister bosses have however been severely damaged by vandals in the sixteenth and seventeenth centuries, and weathering has played its part too in the their deterioration. Various campaigns have been undertaken to repair the damage, even to repaint. One such major repair took place under Professor Tristram in the 1930s, and in the 1980s and 1990s the restoration work has continued. Despite their vulnerability the cloister bosses retain their attractiveness and continue to delight and astonish the viewer with the range of subject and the cunning and zest of the original craftsmen.

The Nave In 1463 fire destroyed the wooden roof of the nave. Bishop Lyhart (1446-72) decided on a stone-vaulted replacement. He took advice probably from Reginald Ely, a Norfolk man from Coltishall, whose work on King's College Chapel had been suspended in consequence

(7) *The beheading of John the Baptist* – (cloister, south walk)

(8) *The Penance of Henry II at the shrine of St Thomas of Canterbury* – (cloister, north walk)

of the house of York replacing the house of Lancaster in 1461. Lierne vaulting was the form adopted, the same used by Ely in the north-east side chapels at King's. This type of vaulting in which many minor ribs were 'tied' together necessitated a great number of keystones, twenty-four to each bay. And there were fourteen bays in all. The grand scheme for the subject of the bosses would not have been chosen by the master mason but by the bishop or the bishop and prior together. The first seven bays starting from the east end of the nave are filled with bosses which tell the story of the Creation of the World (Photo. 1) until the coming of Christ, and the second set of seven bays, ending by the great west window, tell the story of Christ's birth, ministry, Passion, Resurrection, Ascension, and end with the Last Judgement.

Of the twenty-four bosses in each bay, six, three either side of the central transverse rib, are foliate or floral. The centre boss in each bay, larger than the rest, gives the subject for the bay. The rest of the bosses within the bay usually contribute to the story set by the centre boss. For instance, the centre boss in Bay 3 is of Abraham about to sacrifice his son, Isaac, on an altar. The satellite bosses set round the centre boss in stellar pattern depict the following: Rebecca disguising Jacob (Photo. 9); Esau returning from hunting

(9) *Rebecca places a false beard on to the face of her son Jacob to make him 'a hairy man'* – (nave)

(Photo. 10); Abraham entertaining Jehovah's angels (Photo. 11); Rebecca at the well; Abraham's servant holding a horse by the halter as he awaits the outcome of the scene of sacrifice; the same servant on his way to fetch a wife for Isaac;

(10) Esau returns from hunting – (nave)

(11) Abraham entertains an angel – (nave)

Isaac blessing Jacob; Jacob killing a kid; Esau by Isaac's side learning of Jacob's trickery.

The sequence of nave bosses follows a similar story-line as that of the medieval mystery plays which were at their most popular throughout the country in the middle of the fifteenth century. Adam, Noah (Photo. 12), Abraham, Jacob, Joseph, Moses, David are the central themes for the first seven bays. The seven bays treating the New Testament have as their central bosses the Birth of Christ, the Baptism, the Last Supper, the Trial before Pilate, the Crucifixion, the Ascension [this bay includes the representation of the Resurrection (Photo. 13)], and the Last Judgement. Whereas the nave vaulting gives equal space to Old and New Testaments the mystery plays give twice the space to New rather than Old Testament themes; and in the plays there is scant treatment of Jacob and Joseph. But in both art forms the events of the Old Testament are interpreted as prefiguring the events of the New Testament.

Norwich had its own Corpus Christi cycle but alas only one of its plays, the Grocers' play of *Paradise,* has survived in a redacted form. But the N-Town Plays, a major extant cycle of the fifteenth century, almost certainly is of Norfolk provenance. The roof bosses in the nave repeatedly bring to mind the episodes in the drama. It

is not too fanciful to imagine the craftsmen who were carving the bosses having also annually the responsibility of staging the plays.

Bauchon Chapel   The Bauchon Chapel is on the south side of the ambulatory. It was built 1327-29, but it was not until about 1475 that the vaulted ceiling was introduced. The Chapel is dedicated to Our Lady of Pity. The stellar, lierne vaulting is divided into two bays. The centre boss in the southern bay is that of the Assumption of the Blessed Virgin, and the centre boss of the northern bay is that of the Coronation of the Virgin. There are in all 47 bosses in the vaulting and the majority tell the story of the calumniated empress. Such a theme found many versions in the Middle Ages, one of which was Chaucer's Man of Law's Tale in the *Canterbury Tales.* The Norwich version is different in nearly every detail from Chaucer's. The Empress is falsely accused by the Emperor's brother. She is tried, found guilty, and sent to her death. She is rescued by a knight whose brother woos the empress in vain and then 'frames' her for the murder of the knight's son. In exile the Virgin Mary shows her a leaf with the property of healing leprosy. The empress returns to her country unrecognised and heals the two maligning brothers who have been afflicted with leprosy.

(12) Noah builds his ark – (nave)

(13) The Resurrection – (nave)

They confess their sins, and the empress is reconciled to the emperor.

The medieval carvers in the Bauchon Chapel depict most parts of the above story but the haphazard arrangement of the bosses makes for difficult reading. In addition some of the work is of high quality, for instance the empress riding in procession with the emperor with their tall crowns magnificently detailed (Photo. 14), and some is the crude work of an apprentice. Of significance, however, is the introduction of a popular romantic theme in the iconography of the cathedral.

Presbytery The wooden roof of the presbytery was replaced by a magnificent stone vault in about 1480 during the episcopate of Bishop Goldwell (1472-99). It was pitched ten feet higher than the nave vaulting and, because in addition the tall 1360s clerestory windows allow so much more light into the presbytery, the effect is brilliant. The vaulting covers the four bays and the apse. The bosses in their lierne, stellar pattern seem indeed like stars. But the story-telling treatment has been abandoned. Of the 128 bosses 94 are of gold wells, a rebus on the bishop's name (Photo. 15). Others are floral or foliate, and of the five centre bosses three show the bishop's coat of arms and the others are the Virgin in Glory, and the Holy Trinity.

(14) The Empress and the Emperor ride in procession – (Bauchon Chapel)

Transepts A fire in the transepts in 1509 led Bishop Nykke (1501-36) to follow the example of his predecessors and replace the wooden roofing with a lierne stone vaulting. The pattern followed that in the nave and presbytery. Although there was a reversion to story-telling the mode was

(15) A gold well – (presbytery)

(17) Sir William Wingfield and his wife

different. The themes chosen for the north transept were the birth of John the Baptist and the birth of Christ, followed by the adoration of the shepherds and the Magi, the massacre of the innocents and the death of Herod. The themes for the south transept continued with Christ in the Temple with the doctors (Photo. 16), the ministry of John the Baptist and his death, and Christ's calling of his disciples and his early ministry.

There are 75 storied bosses in each transept but they are arranged so that five or six carvings might be given to a single part of the story. For instance the Annunciation is shown by separate bosses of God instructing Gabriel in heaven, by Gabriel leaving the gates of heaven, by his approach to the Virgin Mary, and by his allaying Joseph's fears at what has happened. Small movements of action are dealt with separately such as the Magi riding to Herod's court, meeting Herod, riding away, following the star, approaching the manger, entering, giving their gifts and departing. It is a sculptural model of an animated cartoon.

The transept bosses were the last to be carved. By the time that the bishop who had ordered the work had died, the reformation of the church was in hand and such carvings were beginning to be viewed as fostering idolatry. But the high bosses in the nave, presbytery and transepts escaped the impending vandalism.

(16) Christ with the doctors in the temple –
(south transept)

(18) Samson struggles with a lion

A debt is owed to those bishops of Norwich who successively vaulted cloisters, nave, presbytery and transepts limiting the danger of fire and leaving a legacy of storied bosses that can still be read with wonder today.

Misericords

When Norwich Cathedral was founded in 1096 a Benedictine priory was established at the same time on an adjoining site. It was the monks of this priory who had the responsibility for singing each day the many church offices that were required of such a community. There were eight daily offices excluding Mass. Standing was required for most of the service. Attendance was expected. The first service, prime, might begin according to the time of the year as early as 2.30am, and the last, compline, would be conducted just before an early bed-time. The cathedral was large and draughty and in the winter very cold. The choir, where the monks stood to sing the offices, was furnished in the course of time with screens, canopies, and desks. When choir stalls were introduced here, probably in the thirteenth century, a further facility was introduced to help the aged and infirm. When the seat of the stall was in a tipped-up position a ledge was exposed upon which the monk might rest though seeming still to stand.

By such a means the physical burden of daily attendance of the offices was greatly eased. Such 'mercy' shown the monks was the term transferred to the ledge and it was called by the Latin name for mercy 'misericordia'. And by yet further transference 'misericord' has come to refer to the carving on the supporting corbel under the ledge.

Successive fires in the cathedral destroyed not only wooden roofs but also furnishings. A campaign to renew the choir stalls was planned in the second part of the fourteenth century and accomplished in about 1420. Seventy choir stalls each with misericords were built and placed in the present choir and also at the same height across the transepts. The fire of 1463 occasioned further damage and thirty-five stalls were replaced in about 1480. The fire of 1509 occasioned the replacing of yet more stalls, of which two misericord carvings have survived.

The extant set of the Norwich Cathedral misericords comprises 22 from Bishop Wakering's episcopate (1416-25), 35 from Bishop Goldwell's (1472-99), and 2 from Bishop Nykke's (1501-36). There is one other misericord of a quite different style that probably came from one of the cathedral's chapels. There remain 64 choir stalls 60 of which possess misericord carvings, a rich and rare survival from the Middle Ages.

Bishop Wakering's misericords Although severe damage was inflicted on the choir after a hurricane in 1362 blew down the spire, the complete refurnishing of the choir had to wait for about sixty years. During this period many East Anglian gentry supported such a project, as testified by the presence of their coats of arms on the misericords and elbow-rests. Some such as John Le Strange, William de Ufford, Sir William Wingfield, died before the work was put in hand. Many others died of dysentery or the hand of war during Henry V's 1415 French campaign, such as Richard Courtenay, Bishop of Norwich, Sir Thomas Morley, Sir Robert Berney, and Michael de la Pole, the second Earl of Suffolk.

A salient characteristic of this first phase of carving is the shape of the ledge. It comprises six concave edges whereas the 1480's ledge is characterised by two lobes. The central carving on the

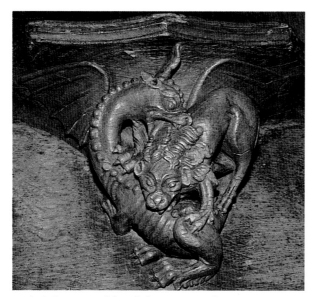

(19) Dragon and lion fighting

(20) Gluttony rides on a sow

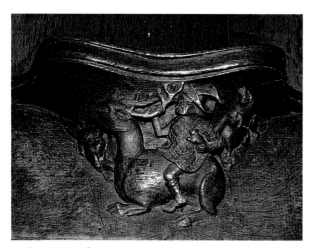

(21) Lust rides on a stag

corbel is balanced by two further carvings, one either side. Sometimes these are formal leaf or floral patterns but very often they reflect the theme of the central carving, for instance the mermaid suckling a lion, with dolphins as supporters devouring their young: the mermaid is a siren that beguiles and destroys.

In this first phase the supporters often depict the coats of arms of the donors, as in the case of John Clere and Denise Wichingham, or the carving of St George flanked by the arms of Sir Thomas Hoo and those of his mother. Sir Thomas Erpingham, a Norfolk man who led the archers at Agincourt, is considered one of the main contributors to the rebuilding of the choir, and his coat of arms is to be seen on one of the elbow-rests. The recurrence of carved representations of the Norfolk gentry lends a poise, dignity and elegance to the craftsmen's work, none more so than that of Sir William Wingfield and his wife Margaret who stand side by side with the wife holding her husband's gauntleted hand (Photo. 17). There are in addition magnificently carved heads of two kings. Perhaps they represent the two Lancastrian kings, Henry IV and Henry V, but it is doubtful whether any copying of their actual features was attempted.

There are a few subjects with a religious significance such as the coronation of the Virgin Mary, Samson struggling with a lion (Photo. 18), St Michael overcoming a seven-headed beast but, apart from the donor references, the main thrust of the carving is directed to animal forms with allegorical import. There are evil-threatening wyverns (two-legged dragons) with outstretched wings and grimacing snouts; there are dragons fighting lions (Photo. 19); a lion in a stand-up struggle with a collared bear; and a naked man assailed by a wyvern, a dragon, and a lion simultaneously. The choice of subject, the imaginative use of the very limited space available, and the skill of the carver all contribute to work of a high order.

Bishop Goldwell's misericords Allegory plays an even stronger part in the 1480's misericord subjects. A wild man with a monstrous club has subdued and chained a lion; a warrior with lance and shield fights with a griffin, a mythical creature

44

with the front part of an eagle and the rear part of a lion; a fool accompanied by a dog and a monkey holds the rear end of a pig and appears to be using the pig's tail as the chanter of a pair of bagpipes; Green Men look out menacingly from their foliate faces. And there is representation of some of the seven deadly sins. Anger rides on a boar showing its tusks. Anger as he sits astride its ridged back strains to draw his sword. Gluttony riding on a fat sow (Photo. 20), has a pot belly himself. A feeding bowl dangles on a cord from his neck; he tips a tankard towards his mouth but the liquour spills down his neck as his hat falls off the back of his head. Lust dressed in a netted tunic (Photo. 21), rides on a stag, clutching its antlers with one hand and holding a squirrel in the other hand. The stag with its horns is a common image of lust. The supporters are on either side monsters whose heads appear in their chests: creatures as mindless as lust. Avarice is carved on one of the elbow-rests as an old man tenaciously clutching a bag of money.

The choir stalls that for many centuries were placed across the transepts were lowered in 1851 and the canopies removed and access was given to the crossing for congregational use. In 1948 six stalls were removed from the transepts: four were placed in the south of the sanctuary acting as sedilia, and two were moved to the north side of the sanctuary. Some of the most exquisite carving can be seen in the sanctuary misericords and elbow-rests.

Unlike the nave and transept roof bosses which consistently represent scriptural subjects as though the medieval mystery plays were being fully illustrated in stone, the misericords give sparse treatment to scriptural themes but depict abundantly the vices and follies of man, reflecting on his animal nature and the struggle he must

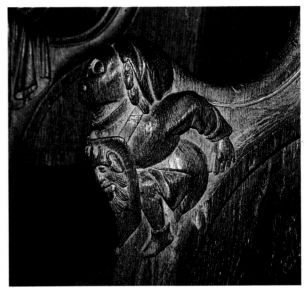

(22) Elbow-rest: a shield-bearer

endure to win salvation. These are the themes of the medieval morality plays.

Norwich Cathedral is fortunate indeed to have retained 60 of its medieval misericords. The vandals have left their mark; but as the misericords were hidden away and their subject matter not on the whole overtly religious the damage they wreaked was not extensive. The remarkable elbow-rests (Photo. 22) have been worn smooth with the caress of many hands, but they too have retained their charm, each scrupulously different and full of latent energy. The craftsmen working on the stalls, because much of the work was out of sight, were not under the close scrutiny of bishop or prior. They were given scope. Their imagination and skill responded to that freedom, and our inheritance is so much the richer.

Photographs by kind permission of *Ken Harvey (Photos. 2, 3, 5-7, 17-22); Michael Trendell (Photos. 4, 8); Julia Hedgecoe (Photos. 1, 9-16).*

In the 12th century when the cathedral was completed by its Norman builders the stone interior would have been richly and brilliantly painted. This, of course, was long before the stone vaults in the nave, transepts and presbytery with their sculptured and painted bosses, replaced the original timber roofs. Traces of medieval decoration can still be seen in places, discovered in the nineteenth century when whitewash, applied largely under Puritan influence, was removed.

The Cathedral chapels

JIM WILSON

Amid the soaring architecture of Norwich Cathedral are six havens of prayer and contemplation, the cathedral's side chapels. Three radiate from the ambulatory, the semi-circular aisle behind the high altar. One extends from the south aisle of the presbytery. The other two lead off the north and south transepts.

Before the Reformation the cathedral had up to fourteen chapels where monks said mass. The six which remain in use combine ancient with modern craftsmanship.

On the north side of the ambulatory is the Jesus Chapel. In Herbert de Losinga's day it was dedicated to the Holy Martyrs. From the middle of the twelfth century to at least the mid-fifteenth century it contained the tomb of the boy-martyr St William of Norwich. Its bulbous shape is unusual. Instead of projecting straight out from the ambulatory, similar to apsidal chapels on the Continent, it is in two sections. The apse is skewed to face due east and a horseshoe shaped extension connects it to the ambulatory. The emphasis in England on east facing altars is probably a throwback from pagan traditions.

The chapel's altar top is a rare example of a medieval sealed mensa. Made from Barnack stone, it was discovered in the floor of the cathedral in 1871. Toolmarks and mouldings on it suggest it is contemporary with the chapel. The purpose of the mensa was to contain relics, a common custom in the Middle Ages although the survival of an altar like this is unusual in England.

The painting which stands on the altar depicts the Adoration of the Magi and was painted in 1480 by Martin Schwarz of Rothenburg. It was given to the cathedral in 1967.

The Jesus Chapel has been skilfully restored in recent years and includes fine oak seating which cleverly uses the Norman wall arcade as its background. Traces of the original wall painting which once decorated much of the cathedral can be seen on the arch and vault.

A curious and rather sad riddle is represented in the inscription on a stone in the floor which records the death of the infant Elizabeth Bacon apparently almost two months before she was born! 'Born April 13th 1736, died February 20th 1736', the inscription reads. The anomaly is explained by the change over from Julian to Gregorian calendar which had the effect of turning back the clock.

At the apex of the ambulatory, the furthest eastern point of the cathedral, is St Saviour's Chapel, a modern addition on old foundations.

The first chapel was begun by Herbert de Losinga in 1096 when he founded the cathedral. It was here the cathedral's foundation stone was laid. Bishop Walter de Suffield demolished

The Adoration of the Magi *on the altar of Jesus Chapel*

The Jesus Chapel

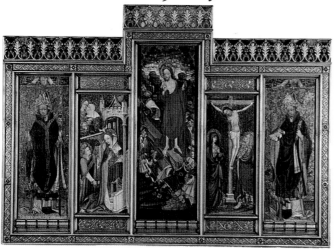

Masterpieces of medieval painting. Top: *St Saviour's Chapel triptych.* Below: *The magnificent Despenser reredos in St Luke's Chapel*

Herbert's chapel in the mid-thirteenth century and replaced it with a much larger Lady Chapel, a fine example of early English Gothic. However, in the 1570's the then Dean, George Gardiner, allowed it to fall in to ruin, stripped the lead from its roof and pocketed the proceeds, plus much other 'loot' from the cathedral and the Close.

Remains of Suffield's Lady Chapel can be seen in the ruins of walls outside and in the elegant pair of arches, enriched with deep mouldings and dogtooth ornamentation, at the entrance to the present day chapel.

The existing chapel was begun in 1930 and was consecrated on May 3rd 1932 as a memorial

to those who died in the First World War. It is now the Regimental Chapel of the Royal Norfolk Regiment and holds the regiment's colours. Battle honours of the regiment round the walls chronicle the history of the rise of the British Empire and record the part played by Norfolk men in many historic campaigns.

The chapel was designed by Sir Charles Nicholson. Its window glass portrays the four East Anglian Saints: Edmund, Julian, Felix and Fursey. The chapel contains the rolls of honour of both world wars, and memorial stones on the floor commemorate those who served in the Regiment since its formation in 1685. One is a memorial to members of the 1st Battalion who fell in the Korean War 1951-52. A bronze plaque recalls the Royal Norfolk's casualties at Kohima where the Japanese advance was halted in 1944.

A group of fine medieval painted panels form the triptych on the altar. They are by Norwich painters of the late fourteenth and early fifteenth centuries. It has been suggested that local artists of the time were producing work comparable with the best of Italian master painters.

These particular panels came from the church of St Michael-at-Plea, Norwich and were moved here in 1954 after restoration by Mr John Brealy in collaboration with the Courtauld Institute. The five individual panels which form the triptych date from between 1385 and 1430.

St Luke's Chapel

Bauchon Chapel

St Catherine's Chapel

The little Norman chapel of St Luke's on the south side of the processional path, mirrors the Jesus Chapel in its horseshoe shape. It was originally dedicated to St John the Baptist but became known as St Luke's because in the fifteenth century it was used by the Guild of St Luke which represented plumbers, and glaziers in the city.

St Andrew's Chapel

This chapel is particularly remarkable because it is a parish church within a cathedral. Following destruction, in 1570, of the church of St Mary-in-the-Marsh, which stood on the south side of the Close, the parishioners were allowed to use this chapel and part of the adjacent aisle as their parish church. They brought with them the font recovered from St Mary's. It is a fine example of a fifteenth century 'Seven Sacraments' font, characteristic of East Anglia. Round the bowl are depicted: Baptism, Confirmation, Ordination, the Eucharist, Marriage (note the bride's fine butterfly head-dress of about 1483) Unction, the Crucifixion, and Penance. Beneath, somewhat battered from the attentions of the Puritans, are ecclesiastical and angelic figures holding emblems. The baton fastened to the wall is the token of office of the parish constable of St Mary's.

The particular treasure of St Luke's Chapel, indeed one of the masterpieces of the cathedral, is the reredos, an outstanding example of the work of Norwich artists of about 1382. The story behind it is equally remarkable. Henry Despenser, Bishop of Norwich (1370-1406) led the attack against the Norfolk version of the Peasant's Revolt in 1381, defeating the rebel leader, John Litester, at North Walsham. Despenser was both a famed warrior-bishop and a priest. After capturing Litester, he sat in judgement upon him and condemned the rebel to death for treason. Then as priest he heard Litester's confession, absolved him and accompanied him to the scaffold to administer a last blessing. Bishop Despenser and leading nobles of the county gave this reredos in gratitude for their victory.

The masterpiece was saved from certain destruction at the time of the Civil War by the simple subterfuge of turning it upside down and disguising it as a table. The ploy was so successful that its secret was not revealed for 200 years. In 1847 it was found in an upstairs room still in use as a table.

The reredos consists of five oak boards pinned together with a moulded frame. It was brilliantly restored by Pauline Plummer in 1958 when the top board and frame, lost at the Reformation, were replaced. The subjects of the painting, in bold jewel-like colours, illustrate the climax of Our Lord's life: the Flagellation, the Way to the

Statue of Our Lady of Pity *by John Skelton, in the Bauchon Chapel*

Photo: E.C.N. Ltd

Cross, the Crucifixion, the Resurrection and the Ascension.

The panels are believed to be the work of Thomas de Okell, Mayor of Norwich, who painted the Wilton Diptych now in the National Gallery. Okell and his son were both artists and it is known they did work for the cathedral. Oak leaves in the background to the Resurrection scene could be a rebus of their name. However, there is conflicting evidence over whether or not a 'local school' of panel painting existed at this time. Consequently art historians regard the place in East Anglian medieval art of the Despenser Retable as something of an enigma.

The Bauchon Chapel of Our Lady of Pity opens off the third bay of the south aisle. It was built between 1327 and 1329, by William Bauchon, who was granarius or corn storekeeper to the Priory. He is mentioned in the priory rolls between 1289 and 1330, as is the cost of building the chapel, £14.17s.4d. – a measure of inflation since the fourteenth century.

The original chapel was altered in about 1470 when the chapel's walls were raised and a vaulted roof added, richly adorned with carved bosses. This work was carried out at the expense of William Sekyngton, advocate in the Consistory Court. His arms appear on vault corbels on the south wall and he himself is portrayed on the central corbel on the west wall.

The vault is in two bays. The central boss of the south bay shows the Assumption of the Blessed Virgin. That of the north bay portrays her Coronation with God the Father, the Son and the Holy Spirit. Most of the other bosses illustrate a story popular in the Middle Ages which when the vault was built had recently been published as part of the 'best seller' of the day – the 'Man of Lawes Tale' in Chaucer's Canterbury Tales.

The chapel was used for many years as the Consistory Court of the Diocese. However, the notorious 1930's trial of the Vicar of Stiffkey over his associations with London prostitutes drew so many people it had to be heard in London, although the vicar's ceremonial 'de-frocking' did take place in the cathedral. In 1968 the chapel was restored to its original use and became the chapel of the Friends of Norwich Cathedral.

In 1964 the chapel's window was fitted with fine modern glass. Named the Benedictine window it depicts leading members of the Benedictine monastic order who helped change the history of Europe, and recalls Benedictine associations with Norwich and East Anglia. Among the subjects portrayed are the shield of St Benet's Abbey, of which the Bishop of Norwich has been titular Abbot since the time of Henry VIII; Bishop Herbert de Losinga illustrating his vision for the completion of Norwich Cathedral; monks assisting in its building; William Bauchon holding in his hand a model of his chapel; the shields of the See of Norwich and of the Cathedral; and St Julian of Norwich with her crucifix and her book 'Revelations of Divine Love'.

The statue of Our Lady of Pity by John Skelton, a former chorister in the cathedral choir, is a fine piece of modern sculpture. The wrought iron screen dividing the chapel from the ambulatory was designed by Sir Bernard Fielden, and made by Mr Eric Stevenson of Wroxham. The painting of the Presentation of Christ in the Temple is by John Opie (1791).

The cathedral's fifth chapel is St Catherine's located at the far end of the south transept. The original building dates from about 1250. There is a chapel on the floor above which was dedicated to St Michael. For many years these two rooms were used as the Sacrist's upper and lower chambers and more recently as the Dean's vestry, but in 1983 the lower room was refurbished and rededicated as a place of quiet prayer and contemplation.

The uncluttered simplicity of the chapel, its modern glass door engraved with quotations from T. S. Eliot's 'Four Quartets' contrasting with the thirteenth century chamber beyond, is remarkably effective.

Occupying a similar position in the north transept is the Norman chapel of St Andrew's restored in memory of Archdeacon Westcott in 1920. Parts of the glass in the early English window date from a visit paid to Norwich by Cardinal Wolsey. The glass was brought here from a room in the Deanery where Wolsey stayed in 1524 when settling disputes during the reign of Bishop Richard Nykke.

The cathedral's 'lost' chapels include St Anne's, which occupied a similar position to the Bauchon Chapel, but projecting from the north aisle. Another which has long disappeared was the Relic Chapel, built in 1398 north of the existing reliquary arch.

Others, no longer used, are at first floor level. The wide upper gallery formed a processional route to them. The unused upper chapels in the transepts are approached via spiral staircases and wall passages.

Seven Sacraments' *font in St Luke's Chapel*

51

St Andrews Norwich Steeple Cup, (1617)

West Acre Flagon, (1674)

North Tuddenham Cup and Cover, (1682)

Hunstanton St Edmund Ciborium, (1923)

Haveringland (Cup) Chalice, (Continental 17th Century)

John Grenville Ciborium (20th Century) Norfolk Museum Service

Great Hockham Alms Dish, (1894)

Photography by
E M Trendell ARPS

Treasury of the Diocese

NIGEL BUMPHREY

THE Treasury was the gift of the Worshipful Company of Goldsmiths, one of many which now grace some of the cathedrals of England. It was designed by the Architect, Stefan Buzas RDI, after many years of discussion and planning, and was opened in 1973 by the Prime Warden of the Worshipful Company, Mr R. F. Vanderpump. The Treasury, designed specifically for church plate, is housed in specially constructed showcases above the ancient Reliquary Arch in the north aisle of the presbytery. This proves to be an ideal place in which to display treasures of the diocese, especially since the original purpose of the arch was probably for the occasional display of 'relics and treasures'.

'The Treasury is a glittering box of glass set high above the aisle to the left of the High Altar' – so states the writer of the *Norwich Silver Trail*. Indeed, the Treasury glistens there above the arch, the light reflecting on the glass and the silver it contains. The silver displayed is exceptional, all coming from the cathedral and from churches throughout the diocese. Often the pieces are returned to their parishes for use at special services and festivals.

With silver spanning nearly 500 years much could be told of the history of the Church. This display shows some of the earliest and finest Pre-reformation patens in the Norwich Diocese. The diocese has a large number of these patens, many of which are still in use in the parishes including one made in 1504, which is still used regularly during Sunday Eucharist. Some of those displayed are of a similar age. The cups, especially the 'Norwich Cups' *(ie those Hallmarked in Norwich)* are a result of the order which went out from the Diocesan Bishops in the 1560's, that chalices should be replaced by communion cups. This was ordered in the Norwich Diocese after the Archbishop's visitation in 1567. The east case shows cups of this period, but many others are still in regular use within their parishes. Norwich

The Diocesan Treasury beneath the medieval painted vault of the reliquary arch

Goldsmiths were largely responsible for carrying out this edict. Their cups are as good as any made in England at that time and even better than most! The bowl of a communion cup is usually bell or beaker shape with the stem capstan or spool, often shaped with a simple moulding in the middle. Of course, some cups are more beautiful than others in shape and proportion, but one needs to remember that in some instances they were re-made from existing chalices – and it is possible so see this. Some parishes hold records of the making of their cup from the original chalice within the Churchwarden's accounts.

For example – the Brockdish Accounts for 1565 state: *'For remaking the Communion Cup at Harleston, 5 shillings and 4 pence (27p today!) besides 6s and 20 (31p today) worth of silver more than the old chalyce weyed.'* The size of the new cup was often determined by the size of the original chalice. The poorer parishes with small chalices had small cups, whereas rich parishes with money to spare indulged in a large grand cup. The paten (lid), which fits the top of the bowl, often shows signs that, like the cup, it has been re-made from an earlier paten.

In 1603 the parishes were ordered to provide flagons in which to bring the wine to the Holy Table. This wine was consecrated for the Communion as well as the cup, in readiness for refilling the cup. Originally pewter flagons were often used, but it soon became fashionable to have silver ones. Not all parishes obeyed this order and so Bishop Wren later ordered that in future *'no wicker bottles or taverne pots be brought to Communion Table'.* Flagons were obviously needed, for on Easter Sunday 1625, at Beccles, 38 quarts of Muskadine wine were bought for Communion! The display in the Treasury shows some splendid flagons, the Diss flagon being the largest.

Some of the church plate is silver gilt, that is a silver base covered with a thin film of gold. In the case of the plate shown in the Treasury, it is fire gilt – now an illegal practice and so modern plate is electrogilded. The silver gilt flagons, patens, cups and almsdish belonging to Oxnead are worthy of note, because of their size and quality and their association with the Paston family. The flagon belonging to West Acre, made in 1607, is quite exceptional, as are some of the cathedral flagons.

The high standard of craftsmanship of the goldsmith and engraver is evident throughout. Of particular note is the engraving on the West Acre flagon; the Illington Caudle cup; some of the patens, and in particular the Steeple cup belonging to St Andrew's Church, Norwich. The work of Continental goldsmiths, as seen in the Haveringland cup, would give the present day goldsmith food for thought! However, the 20th century is represented by some very fine work by Omar Ramsden (the Hunstanton ciborium) and John Grenville (the set lent by the Castle Museum which can be seen in the west case).

I am sure the reader will want to visit the Treasury and look at the magnificent silver displayed there which covers 650 years of the 900 years of the Diocese. Each piece is unique and has its own fascination – for example, work out the names of the twelve stones in the remarkable Great Hockham Alms dish which follow the order given in Revelations XXI verses 19 and 20. Then pause, and think about the paten from Hunstanton which was made and marked in Paris at the time of Napoleon – what a story that piece could tell!

The Treasury is not the only place in Norwich where such fine examples of church plate can be seen. The Castle Museum, the St Peter Mancroft Treasury, and St Peter Hungate are all worthy of a visit.

A fascinating area, and one which can impart much of the history of the 900 years of the diocese, are the pieces of silver to be found elsewhere in the country but are not now within the possession of the diocese. In Canterbury, the Tenison cup bequeathed by Thomas Tenison, Archbishop of Canterbury, son of the Rev John Tenison, Rector of Mundesley, to Dr Charles Trimnel, Bishop of Norwich can be seen in the Museum. Also, at Trinity Hall, Cambridge, is a cup, known as the Founder's Cup, which according to tradition, was given to Trinity Hall by William Bateman, Bishop of Norwich in 1344.

THE PELICAN LECTERN

The Cathedral's medieval pelican lectern is probably of Flemish craftsmanship, dating from the late fourteenth or early fifteenth century. It is made of latten rather than brass. Its claws and the young fledgelings were stolen centuries ago, and the figures of a bishop, priest and deacon at the base and the lectern's lion feet are later additions. The origin of the lectern is based on the widely held medieval belief that the pelican slayed its young and then brought them back to life by tearing at its breast and shedding its lifeblood upon them, symbolising man's fall and redemption.

The Cathedral bells

The cathedral tower contains five bells, hung there in the restoration following the fire of 1463. In recent times they have been re-hung 'dead', to allow them to be chimed but not swung. The chiming, every quarter hour, is controlled by an electronic clock.

The bells were cast in the late fifteenth century by the Norwich foundry of Brasyers. Four bear Latin inscriptions. The tenor, largest of the five, is 41½ inches in diameter and weighs about 12 hundredweight. When chimed they echo the Plainsong tones sung below them during the centuries.

It is known that between 1662 and 1761, the bells were rung in the traditional manner about six times a year.

Access to the Belfry is by wall passages and spiral stone stairs, the steps and ancient wooden doors worn by use through the years.

Other larger bells were originally hung in a campanile or bell tower, a separate building situated in the Upper Close near the Erpingham Gate. Bishop Eborard built the first campanile, but it was largely destroyed in the riot of 1272 when the citizens accused the Prior's men of using it as a vantage point from which to fire on the city. It was rebuilt about 1304 and was demolished in 1570.

Above: *The bell chamber in the crossing tower approached by a well trodden spiral staircase* (below)

Photos: Ken Harvey

The spire windlass

Before the invention of modern lifts and mechanical hoists, timber and other building materials had to be raised by hand into the spire of the cathedral during maintenance and repairs. Hoisting machines, described in some contemporary accounts as 'engines', survive in a few English cathedrals. Some were operated like a tread wheel with a man walking inside to provide the motive power. A hand-operated wheel and windlass survives in the base of the spire at Norwich. It dates from the seventeenth or early eighteenth century and is made of two circular discs of elm fitted to a shaft and supported on a stout timber frame. Hand grips are mounted between the discs and bolted in place like the spokes of a huge ship's wheel. Some idea of its size can be gained by the fact that the horizontal spokes each side are at the operator's eye-level. A device like this provided a clear advantage in hoisting relatively light, but frequently needed, building materials during repairs and maintenance.

THE DEAN'S INSTALLATION

The Very Rev. Stephen Platten was installed as Dean of Norwich on September 23rd 1995. He took his place at the appointed stall in the medieval choir where the Priors and Deans of Norwich Cathedral have had their seat for the past 900 years. Dean Platten is the 36th incumbent since the New Foundation in 1538, when the priory was dissolved after 500 years of monastic rule. The last Prior of Norwich, William Castleton, became the first Dean. His portrait hangs in the cathedral library.

The Bishop is the head of the diocese; the Dean is responsible for the cathedral; and the High Steward is the leading lay advisor. Although Dean Platten is the 36th Dean only 35 clerics have held the post. John Salisbury was appointed twice – 1539-53 and 1560-71. In 1553 he was deprived of his office when Mary came to the throne, and subsequently re-installed when Elizabeth I succeeded her.

Dean John Sharpe (1681-89) is reputed to have confirmed 1,600 people in one day – surely a record since unmatched. He was succeeded by Henry Fairfax (1689-1700). An incumbent who followed soon after, Humphrey Prideaux (1702-24), had little respect for Fairfax under whom he had served in the office of Prebendary. Dean Prideaux recorded that Fairfax 'comes little to church and never to the Sacrament... once a year he will offer to preach... and as soon as the people see him in the pulpit, they all get out of the church... his whole life is that of pipe and pot.'

The Deans who served longest in office were Joseph Turner (1790-1828) and his immediate successor, the Hon George Pellew (1828-66). Edward Meyrick Goulburn, the next Dean (1866-89), left detailed handwritten diaries of his years in Norwich which are now preserved in the cathedral library. Goulburn generously used his own personal wealth to maintain and improve the cathedral fabric. A prolific author, he published a translation of Bishop Herbert de Losinga's letters and sermons. Dean William LeFroy (1889-1909) introduced the cathedral's first carol service in 1890 and oversaw a major refurbishment of the nave and the choir, including completion of the uncovering of the bosses from their eighteenth century coat of whitewash.

Extreme left: *At the climax of the service, the Bishop annoints and blesses the new Dean at the ancient high throne*

Left: *Dean Stephen Platten speaks from the pulpit following his installation*

THE LADY JULIAN

St Julian lived in Norwich as an anchoress and mystic during the fourteenth century. She was the author of one of the great classics of spiritual literature, the first known book written by an English woman. For forty years she lived in almost total seclusion in a cell attached to the chancel of St Julian's Church, Norwich.

St Julian was born in 1342 and probably studied at the Benedictine Convent at Carrow. In May of 1373, during a severe illness, she witnessed sixteen visions of Christ's Passion. She later described what she had seen as 'real, life-like, horrifying and dreadful'. As a result of this experience she applied to Bishop Despenser to join the Order of Recluses. For twenty years she meditated in her sealed cell on the meaning of the visions which

had appeared to her, finally recording her conclusions in her book 'Revelations of Divine Love'. Her words have brought comfort to many in suffering and adversity throughout the centuries.

In 1980 the Church of England included Julian in its Calendar of Saints. Although St Julian's Church was virtually destroyed in air raids on Norwich in 1942, it has been rebuilt with a reconstruction of the cell where Mother Julian was confined for forty years of her life. In the Middle Ages pilgrims came to Norwich for spiritual counsel from her in her cell. The rebuilt cell, now furnished as a chapel, remains a place of pilgrimage for visitors from all over the world.

St Julian's cell as reconstructed following bomb damage in 1942

The Diocese today

TREVOR REID

I T is often difficult for those with a glassy-eyed view of the ancient rites and equally ancient buildings of the Church of England, to grasp the notion that all is not ancient – many areas are now very modern.

When I moved from more than three decades of secular journalism to putting forward the point of view of the Church, I left an industry screaming its way into the next millennium. Caxton was a long time ago, the media has moved on. The Reformation was a long time ago – the Church in England has moved on.

The Norwich Diocese has a modern approach to the future. Its leaders and managers are well aware of today's problems, changes and challenges and they are tackling them. They are equally ready to identify and solve those that lie ahead. But the diocese and its supporters are facing the future and – dare we say it – often proving more effective than many of our counterparts elsewhere.

The diocese covers a vast tract of East Anglia – 1804 square miles – very nearly the geographic area of Norfolk, losing a bit to Ely in the West and South, but winning some ground from St Edmundsbury and Ipswich in the East.

Within these diocesan boundaries live 783,000 people.

The 647 parish churches – including the largest collection of medieval, listed churches anywhere in the world, 600 of them – provide the diocese and the parishes with a permanent challenge to keep the roof sound and the weather out.

And while we are relating facts and figures, there are 216 benefices, 582 parishes and 224 clergy – although this latter figure varies year by year.

The upkeep is always a worry for both diocesan managers and parishioners. And there sometimes comes a day when all good efforts to keep a little-used medieval gem for parish purposes have to come to an end. Another life can nearly always be found for the building so that its vital place in the local community can continue.

In the City of Norwich for instance – once the proud boast that it had a church for each week of the year and come to that an equal boast of a pub for each day – we see the ancient buildings being used as arts centres, puppet theatres, Scout headquarters, antique showrooms, cinemas, rest, community and advice centres. All benefiting the various groups they now serve in their fresh life.

Backing and support comes from many quarters. Most is raised, gathered, sweated for locally, grants come from various sources – conservation trusts, historic preservation funds, the Norfolk Churches Trust, a society that takes an interest in round tower churches and even English Heritage.

Recently we have seen one rural church receive a grant from the National Lottery Heritage Fund to help convert it to an arts and exhibition centre at South Walsham near the Broads.

But even support can mean battles. Bishop Peter is campaigning in the House of Lords for an end – or at least a reduction – to the addition of VAT to repair, renovation and preservation work on ancient listed buildings. He has impressive cross-party support in the Lords to remove this mill-stone from the neck of those trying to keep our heritage safe for future generations.

In many cases the cost of the VAT bill on materials and work for restoration and repair, far outweighs the grant given from government cash via English Heritage.

But the Church is not about buildings – although they take much time and worry – it is about people.

The diocese can be viewed as an ancient grouping of like-minded individuals or as a modern movement moulding the future with others in mind.

It is a multi-million pound organisation, has district offices in all towns, villages and hamlets in the county. It has its 250 full time representatives available 24-hours a day, seven days a week to serve the people.

And each and every week it can gather together over 50,000 people to take part in its organised services. I am sure Norwich City would be delighted to have that number each week filling its terraces.

But moving forward into the future means change, and often change can be difficult. Parishes amalgamate, always at the request of the parishioners and never from outside pressures, taking into account the changing patterns of worship and mobility.

It means professional attitudes by diocesan staff, officers and managers, and by clergy. No longer can the Church afford just to mumble its hopes and fears into a prayer book each Sunday.

Modern systems now help to take the load. Diocesan House at Easton has its fair share of computers and the technical assistance of the 1990s. Modern communications are now very much to the fore, outgoing and positive relations with the media are vital and now part of a full time mission in the diocese.

Nowadays it is no longer possible for a modern bishop to comment through a third party that he has nothing to say on a vital topic, or issue a few words on a piece of paper to placate sound-bite led journalists. He must be the man in the front line of media response, and to say it in person, in glorious colour on our news pages and on television.

The diocese has clergy and lay people working professionally in radio – a producer with BBC Radio Norfolk and a professionally-led team of volunteers with Broadland FM. They are all adding to the awareness and vision of the church in the larger, and sometimes less responsive world of the electronic media.

As Diocesan Communications Officer, on my office wall I have pinned up a cutting from a journalist's magazine I take.

With the Red Sea parted and the sturdy travellers trudging through into the distance, dwarfed by the mountainous walls of water, Moses has dropped back to have a few words with Caleb strolling along behind in his Hawaiian shorts and carrying his surfboard. 'Caleb', he says, 'I don't think you completely grasp the seriousness of our situation.'

Our answer to Moses is simple. 'Yes we have'. We are well along the road to ensure that we have a modern, responsive, caring and professional Church within the Diocese of Norwich.

If only we could look one hundred years ahead to the time when those following come to celebrate one thousand years of the diocese and cathedral. What will be their opinion of the way we have cared for the Living Church in Norfolk?

The Diocese of Norwich and its Deaneries

Thetford School BY DAVID SEYMOUR

Herbert de Losinga received royal nomination to the East Anglian diocese in 1090 after three years as abbot of Ramsey and was consecrated bishop by Thomas, Archbishop of York probably at an Epiphany ceremony in 1091. His cathedral, Great St Mary's, was on the site now occupied by Thetford Grammar School.

For Thetford Grammar School the letter of Herbert concerning Dean Bund is clearly of the first importance. In place of the inferences which must be the basis when considering the school's Anglo-Saxon origins, this letter provides the first documentary evidence of its existence. The usual date attributed to the letter is 1114 and as such Bund appears as the first of the headmasters recorded on the roll in the library of the school.

Herbert wrote: 'Know that I have restored to Bund, the dean, his schools at Thetford as completely and advantageously as he ever held them; and I order that no other schools shall be held there except his, or such as he has allowed to be held'.

The kind of education provided in Bund's schools and in those of Herbert in Thetford, prior to his transference of the see to Norwich, can be deduced from a reading of Herbert's letters relating to the educational provision he made at Norwich. Two pupils received his particular notice: William and Odo. Herbert reproved his pupils for being sluggish and for spending too long on the easy parts of the syllabus. One letter, in particular, demands of the students a professional and dedicated approach to the work: '…you write nothing unless you are goaded to it; say nothing unless closely questioned. You might, at least once, break forth on your own account. You are the most indolent and sluggish of youths. How long will you disgrace yourselves with these infantile dribblings? … It is only with great effort of will and purity of mind that wisdom can be obtained'.

He paid careful attention to the marking of his pupils' work as this extract makes clear; 'In the first line you make a silly beginning … in line nine you use a wrong word … in line twenty-two your rhyme has no reason …'.

It is clear from his letters that Herbert understood the value of education and that he was diligent in seeking the best from his pupils. He left a lasting legacy to Thetford by ensuring the continuance of a school with claims to be one of the oldest educational foundations in the country.

The shrine of St Edmund

When Bishop Herfast transferred the bishopric to Thetford he may have regarded it as a temporary arrangement. There is evidence he planned eventually to locate it at Bury St Edmunds Abbey, one of the four or five richest in the country and the site of the shrine of a man who was both King of East Anglia and a martyr. Herfast was involved in a bitter dispute with Abbot Baldwin of Bury. Although Herfast had been the Conqueror's chaplain, Baldwin proved the more influential. He travelled to Rome to gain the Pope's approval in declaring Bury Abbey exempt from all episcopal control, save obedience to Canterbury, a decision the king supported.

After 1081 it became increasingly inevitable the see could not remain at Thetford on the very edge of the Liberty of Bury St Edmunds. Nevertheless, when Baldwin's magnificent new abbey church, a full fifty feet (15.75m) longer and ten feet (3.15m) wider than Norwich Cathedral, was ready in 1095 for St Edmund's shrine to be moved to it from the original church built during the reign of Cnut, Herbert de Losinga tried to participate in the ceremony. But the saint's liberty was maintained and the Bishop of Winchester was chosen to officiate instead.

In 1101, in the foundation charter for Norwich Cathedral, Herbert claimed Hoxne in Suffolk, which had been the site of the old southern seat of the Diocese, as the scene of St Edmund's martyrdom by the Danes in the nineth century. At the same time he changed the dedication of the bishop's old manor church at Hoxne from Ethelbert, the eighth century East Anglia king and martyr who had a genuine association with the area, to St Edmund. No doubt Herbert hoped to break the monopoly Bury Abbey held over pilgrims to the saint's shrine. Hoxne Priory was established by monks from Norwich, and became a dependent cell of Norwich Cathedral Priory.

In 1107 Herbert made a final attempt to revive the long-standing claims of the Bishops of East Anglia. He set out for Rome hoping to win the Pope's agreement. But he was taken prisoner in France and forced to use the money, with which it is said he had planned to purchase jurisdiction over Bury St Edmunds Abbey, as a ransom payment to secure his release.

Restoring a masterpiece

Pauline Plummer, who expertly repaired and restored the Despenser retable in 1958, found evidence that the masterpiece was used, upside down, as a table in the cathedral's plumber's workshop during part of its 'lost' two centuries.

She found the length of the face of the retable had been sprinkled with splashes of red lead, in blobs. 'From the disposition of these', she wrote, 'it is clear that there was no deliberate attempt to deface. In a few places they had been smeared into long threads before drying. There were also traces of white lead and a green copper residue; all of which tends to confirm the theory that the panel was used as a table in the cathedral plumbery.'

Describing her reconstruction of the woodwork and replacement of the missing section at the top of the retable, Pauline Plummer wrote: 'The original dimensions of the retable cannot be known for certain. However, calculations based on the arrangement of the pastiglia and glass panels on the frame, and the minimum height necessary to complete the central figure of the Crucifixion, make it appear likely that there was a further plank of about 10 in. in width and that the upper edge of the panels was straight. Accordingly, the structure was completed to conform to those calculations.'

Recalling her renewal of the paintwork, she wrote, 'The head of Christ in the central panel was reconstructed in egg tempera on a gesso ground and the pastiglia background on the lower part of the panel was continued. A gap of about 2.6 cm. was left between the old and new sections of this pastiglia, but to do this in the case of the painting of the head was not practicable. Here the new work was carried right down to the edge of the surviving paint. The tops of the other four panels were dabbed with gesso and colour to match areas of wood where the paint had come off.'

Bishop's Lynn and Gt Yarmouth

Herbert de Losinga was not only the benefactor of Norwich. Norfolk's two main towns and seaports owe their early prominence to him. De Losinga conceived the plan of completing three great churches to dominate his diocese. In the centre, the cathedral at Norwich. To the east, St Nicholas' at Great Yarmouth. And on the western boundary, St Margaret's at Lynn. Indeed, until about 1536 Lynn was known as Bishop's Lynn. It only became King's Lynn in deference to Henry VIII at the Dissolution.

De Losinga established the church and priory of St Margaret's Lynn in the late eleventh century almost on the foreshore of the Len, a lake or saltings which shrank in size as the town grew. He endowed it richly and established a market on Saturdays and a fair at the feast of St Margaret. But the priory remained subordinate to the priory at Norwich and it was Norwich who appointed Lynn's Priors.

In the twelfth century Lynn grew rapidly as a port. Around 1125 Bishop Eborard built a chapel at Bishop's Lynn dedicated to St James, and his successor Bishop William de Turbe laid out an extension to the town between 1146 and 1173, incorporating a further market, now known as the Tuesday Market Place. De Turbe established another chapel dedicated to St Nicholas. It is not surprising Lynn became known as Bishop's Lynn as a result of its powerful episcopal benefactors. Before the Norman conquest it had existed as scarcely more than a humble settlement.

When the Normans arrived Great Yarmouth was only just beginning to emerge as a small town from the original tiny fishing community established on an island of sand and shingle in the estuary into which the Yare, Waveney and Bure flowed. Herbert de Losinga founded his priory and the church of St Nicholas there soon after 1100. He was also responsible for the huge market place on the south side of the church. For the Normans religion and commerce went hand in hand. Yarmouth expanded rapidly in the twelfth century, the herring fishing and North Sea trade playing an important part in its growth, and by 1334 it was ranked sixth in wealth among English towns.

Little Snoring: A fascinating outline – and a textbook in miniature of architecture in stone

The never-ending story

For CHARLES ROBERTS, medieval churches in general and those
of Norfolk in particular are an endless source of fascination and delight.
Here he explains why – and takes us on a gentle ramble to
some of his favourite examples.

IMAGINE a late winter afternoon, grey, the light fading, and a remote rural church with only a couple of farms distantly in view.

I'm there doing research for the set of three volumes which D. P. (Sam) Mortlock and I wrote together to bring to as wide a public as possible our keen enthusiasm for our vast heritage of medieval churches in Norfolk.

Even as I'm in the church it gets darker. I'm far from home and don't want to have to come back again. So I go to my car to get a torch – and continue in its light my notes on wall-paintings and wood-carving, on memorials and screen, on architectural detail and the niceties of piscina and sedilia.

I'm entirely at ease, here, alone, in a near-dark church…until I hear, outside, the barely perceptible sound of footsteps on gravel, the footsteps of someone trying not to be heard.

I freeze – and wait. The footsteps, cautious and, to me now, sinister, scrape across the tiles of the porch. Seconds pass. Suddenly, unnaturally loud, the latch of the door echoes upward…and the great medieval door is pushed slowly, slowly, inward, keening on its hinges.

As I clutch my clipboard to my hammering chest, I discern the figure of an old man, straight out of a Victorian print – and pointing straight at me a very businesslike 12-bore. At his side, a no-nonsense dog, lips curled over teeth.

For what seems like minutes we stare at each other. Then his eyes sweep the church, and come back to me. He breaks the silence…. 'Nice da-ee', he say in broad Narfolk.

It's been a horrid day, cold, windy, drizzly, grey. But not for a moment am I going to disagree with this apparition. 'Ye-es, yes, it is', I stutter.

'Saw yu arrive', he says. 'Then you went back to yo'car. Thought I'd better check. We bin in a muddle in this here church with things stolen. You never can tell. So what would you be doing here then….?'

I quote that story because it serves for me to illustrate the fierce caring, the very real love, which surrounds our village churches. And how right was that old boy, in this age of burglaries and vandalism of churches, to be suspicious of 'furriners'.

Maintaining those buildings in the 1990s is an immense burden and responsibility. There are those, clergy and laymen alike, who ask why we should bother to preserve them at all. They are, they say, just buildings, and draughty. uncomfortable buildings too, as often as not, expensive if not impossible to heat and more expensive still to care for. Is not the care of souls, they ask rhetorically, more important than the preservation of bricks and mortar?

Of course they have a point, no-one could disagree with that. But the simple truth is that our medieval churches are more than just buildings. Each one is a living history of its own village, a part of the history of its county and country, a repository of artistic and historic treasures.

And even for those who do not attend services as a matter of course, save for the inevitable hatches, matches and despatches, it is the spiritual heart of the community, a potent symbol of continuance and permanence in a changing, impermanent world.

At home I have the inestimable privilege and never-failing pleasure of looking across a paddock at the modest little round flint tower of the parish church. Always I feel humbled by it, for it has stood there for full one thousand years. The church attached to it has been rebuilt, altered, extended and cared for by generations of loving people throughout that millennium.

That is the inheritance we seek to preserve.

To appreciate our ancient churches to the full you need to 'speak the language' of the buildings and their varied contents; and helping everyone to do just that was one of the principal motivations of Sam Mortlock and I in the way we presented our material in *The Popular Guide to Norfolk Churches*.

We did not approach it as scholars or experts – but as enthusiasts, whose chief satisfaction is to share with others the pleasure, the excitement, the sense of discovery, we find in the many-faceted world of the medieval church. The same stimulus urges me on with the occasional church tours – a coach load of no more than 25, so we can gather round every merest detail – which I lead to specific sets of churches, chosen to span the centuries of changing styles and changing churchmanship.

Salle: A Green Man, age-old pagan symbol of fertility, long-absorbed into Christian imagery

'A goldmine for church enthusiasts' is how David Durant describes Norfolk's 659 medieval churches in his book *'The Good Church Guide'*.

The county has no fewer than 119 round tower churches, 78 of them pre-Conquest. Over 70 Norfolk churches have Norman craftsmanship in them. But the glory of the county in terms of church architecture are the fifteenth century churches built on the profits of the wool trade. They are distinguished by their huge expanse of window allowing the light to flood in illuminating the workmanship of their fine carved roofs.

To the uninformed eye, a church is a church is a church… they all look very much the same. To appreciate them to the full one needs, as I indicated a moment ago, to 'speak the language' of the buildings and their varied contents.

So, the first move is to crack the architectural code. After that comes the rewarding pleasure for Interested Everyman of being able to spot for himself when a church was built, altered, extended… to know to what purposes surviving furnishings and fittings were put in the past – and what we can interpret from them in the present.

Go inside and roofs, when you know what to look for, take on a new significance and the textbook names take on meaning… arch braced, king-posts, hammer-beamed, double hammer-beamed….

A carving of a pelican, driving its beak into its own breast, becomes a tale in itself and a fascinating allegory of Christian belief.

A faded painting of a previously unheard-of saint steps out of obscurity to reveal amazing symbolism and story. A fantastical head of a man with tendrils growing from his mouth and haloing his head – the Green Man – looking down at us from column or roof, links millennia of ancient belief with medieval Christianity… and reminds us of how Man today is plundering and destroying his planet.

A dusty blocked stairway in a wall, or a puzzling arch or oblong set into the wall to the north of the high altar, leads on to a vivid flight back through the imagination to medieval days of mystery and worship. An ancient wall painting, lively and mischievous as a Giles cartoon, mocks the sin of gossip – and lightly leaps the centuries.

Carvings in wood and stone and brass and images in paint and glass reflect hat and gown fashions of four and five centuries ago, as eagerly followed and quickly forgotten then as are fashionable nonsenses today. Low on a wall, a painted cross in a circle, or one carved with delicate care,

Opposite, top: *The soaring beauty of Salle, cathedral of the fields; and* below, *South Walsham, light and charm – and memories of Cromwell's tyranny*

Blakeney: High on its ridge overlooking the sea – with a second tower which served as a lighthouse

take us back even further to the day, perhaps seven centuries ago, when a bishop touched that spot with holy oil to consecrate the building....

At South Walsham the medieval screen reminds us that there was serfdom and slavery in these gentle Norfolk acres. Blakeney Church recalls for us, in its registers, that this little town – but a thriving port then – provided Elizabeth I with three ships against the Spanish armada in 1587. At Great Snoring a poignant memorial records the death of three brothers in 1710 who all 'fell to the same shaft from the quiver, namely smallpox', bringing home to us the epidemic horrors of earlier days.

In Dunston Church a charming epitaph evokes an image of a true Lady Bountiful in times when charity meant personal caring rather than State handouts....

'...Her bounty like an hidden spring was only visible in its Effects, And the glad hearts of those who were refreshed by its streams....'

Susan Long, the subject of those poetic words, must have been a lovely lady in character.

And obviously lovely in appearance as well as in spirit was the young wife of a broken-hearted husband who, at Witton-by-Walsham, expressed his radiant love when she died in an inscription of lyrical beauty which balances on the poignant line....

'She looked like nature in the world's first spring...'

From the other end of life, a rector of Little Snoring quietly led his flock in that quiet village and when, at a venerable age he moved on to the next stage of his pilgrimage, his parishioners inscribed for posterity upon his tombstone in the chancel the affectionate tribute that he was a parish priest...

'...as good perhaps as ever lived'.

Again and again we are thus reminded that our medieval churches are not just ancient masonry, ancient repositories of dead history, but special places, alive and vibrant with the voices of the people who built, cared for and loved them, and who worshipped there through the ages.

Little Snoring St Andrew perfectly reflects these influences. It is among my own especial favourites in Norfolk, fascinating in outline as you approach it, intriguing in detail and – once one has learned to 'speak the language' of architecture, as I noted earlier – a little treasure house of styles through the centuries.

The round tower stands separated by a few feet from the main body of the church, and topped by a curious and delightful little 'cap' (added about two centuries ago) which looks like an elegant pidgeon-cote in a gentleman's park.

It is a Saxo-Norman tower, on whose east side there are the remains of a Norman arch which led into the original church, which has long since disappeared. But when it was taken down, for whatever reason, why wasn't its replacement put in the same place? Why build instead a few paces northwards?

But that is what happened, and not in one operation either. First came a small nave. Was it then extended eastward as the outside masonry on the south side might indicate? Certainly the lovely and sublimely simple chancel came slightly later, about 1250.

Before going inside, let's walk around the outside to begin to discover just what a revelatory little building this is.

Starting from just north of the porch, we see Norman 'slit' windows, tall and narrow like arrow embrasures in a castle, and placing us in the 12th century. At the corner, look at the chunks of stone which form the corner edge, holding together the flint walls. These are 'long and short' which usually indicates Saxon work – but here points to local masons under Norman employers doing what their fathers did!

In the west end there's a fine window in the *reticulated* style – that is, with delicate lacey tracery, from the Latin *reticulus,* a lace bag – which places us around the years 1320-30. Move on to the north side: and to a succession of Norman, Early English (13th century), Decorated (first half of 14th century), Perpendicular (from second half of 14th century to the end of the 15th century) and Tudor (16th century).

So why all these different styles in so small and rural a building? The answer perhaps is that there was never enough money here to make major changes or to rebuild – but at least a bow was made to each new era through minor alterations and additions.

As we move clockwise around the exterior, pause to look at the round clock-like circle with numerous 'hands' radiating from a central hole, which is carved in the stonework of the chancel south-east window. This is a scratch, or mass dial, probably dating from the 13th century – a marker peg was placed in the hole, and each time its shadow (when there was any sun!) reached one of the radiating lines, it was time for an office or mass. Count the number of lines and consider how busy a place was a medieval church.

Back now to the porch, and a wonderful touch of eccentricity. The porch itself, in its

Above: *Saxon simplicity at Gt Dunham – and more to come inside.* Below: *A clean-lined Norman survival at Kenninghall – and within, a direct echo of Elizabeth I*

South Creake: A glory of angels and a church full of treasures

priceless legacy, in which one man's quirky vision has overridden the style book and, centuries on, speaks to us with the authentic voice of a canny Norfolk craftsman.

Walk in now to a cool, calm interior where time is slowed. A massive and rather fine Norman font confronts us. Then a fresh view of Little Snoring's amazing display of window styles.

The eye is led on to the unadorned grace of the Early English chancel arch, built about 1250, and on into the light and refreshingly uncluttered chancel of the same date. The three great lancet-shape windows in the east wall, which look so plain from outside, are here brought into a beautiful pattern and unity by bounding them, and tying them together, with lovely pencil slim shafts, a small triumph of rustic artistry.

To the right, there's an angle piscina and a sedilia. The piscina, 'angled' between wall and window embrasure, was used by the priest to wash the sacred vessels after the mass. Look closely, and it has a miniature central 'sink', carved like a flower, and a drain to release the water. Water which had touched the sacred vessels during the mass had to go back into consecrated ground – so the drain

rough simplicity, dates from about 1300. But the inner door is something very different. Here we have to surmise that the mason cannibalised from somewhere else a round-headed Norman doorway with bold zig-zig ornamental carvings, supported by pretty little capitals from that period around 1200 when the Norman style was being overtaken by the new Gothic, with its pointed arches.

'So', said our mason, 'we're going to go pointed!' And with more determination than art, he pressed and bullied his round-arch materials into something approaching a Gothic shape, keyed together at the point with an oddly disturbing, rather pagan carved head. The overall result is somehow Eastern, altogether individual – and a

Little Snoring: Serene and timeless, with a bold Norman font

Opposite, top: *Edingthorpe, the perfect small rural church;* and below, *Gt Walsingham, a model of the high Decorated style, and a wealth of 15th century pews*

North Tuddenham: Home to very unusual saints and much remarkable ancient stained glass

Gt Walsingham St Peter: Superb nave and tower of the 14th century – and a chancel in romantic ruins

Attlebridge: Distinctive, slim-line tower, and a low side window to catch the eye

runs directly into the church's foundations.

Sedilia provided seats for the clergy. Usually there are three seats, though there can be more (there are five at St Nicholas' in Gt. Yarmouth), either on the same level or 'graduated' at different levels.

Here sat the priest; the deacon, who read the gospel; and the sub-deacon, who read the epistle.

Over the door through which we came in to St Andrew's there is a special treasure, a rare Royal Arms of James II. James ruled for only three years, was hugely unpopular because of his Roman Catholicism and (what seems so reasonable now) his efforts to give his faith freedom and toleration in these islands, and was booted out at the 'Glorious Revolution' in 1688. Thus his Arms in churches are rarely seen. Just up the road in Great Snoring they have what appears to be a James II set. In fact it's a James I Arms, to which penny-watching church wardens merely had another 'I' added for the new reign.

But why are Royal Arms placed in our churches? The answer goes back to Elizabeth I. Following her father Henry VIII's break with Rome, appalling vandalism was carried out during his reign and that of his son, the boy-king Edward VI, including the tearing out of screens which separated chancel from nave – all in the cause of destroying 'popish superstition'.

Elizabeth, that intellectual lady who disliked excess and favoured stability in government and state, stopped all that, and ordered that not only should screens be replaced, but that over them, within the curve of the chancel arch, her Royal Arms should be set up. Should you visit Kenninghall St Mary in the south of the county, you'll see just such a coat, painted on its arch shape, but set up now in the north aisle.

Elizabeth's instruction on the placing of the Arms was forgotten as the years progressed. But the habit of placing them in our churches has survived to today.

I have stayed so long with this one small church because it teaches us, in its own modest way, so much that one may meet with in any of several hundred churches across county and diocese – variety and styles of architecture through six centuries, mass dials, piscinas, sedilia, Royal Arms.

South Lopham and its wonderful tower – Next to the cathedral, the grandest piece of Norman architecture in the county

Bale: Fine medieval glass, crafted in Norwich in the 15th century

Let us move across country a few miles to Great Walsingham St Peter, where the process can continue. The beauty of this superb building is that it is all of an architectural piece, being built around 1330-40. That means that it is in the height of the Decorated style – the reticulated pattern, which we met earlier. But its chancel has long since been a ruin – though a romantic one. One of its special details is there still to see – a small window opening, low down on the south side.

This is a low side window, a facet of medieval churches whose true use is still disputed today. I believe that it was there so that, during the mass, at the moment of the elevation of The Host, a priest could extend an arm through the open window and ring a handbell so that those within hearing, in the village or working in the fields, could stop for a moment, cross themselves, and thus, in spirit, be one in the celebration of the mass.

Another option is that openings like this were leper windows, through which lepers could peer during the service. In medieval England, there were strict laws governing the movements of lepers, which makes this version nonsensical.

The Norfolk churches of Attlebridge, Saxthorpe and Burlingham St Andrew have good complete examples. But the best one I know is at Melton Constable.

Great Walsingham St Peter has a wonderful treasure, a superb set of 15th century benches, with imaginatively carved ends. There's a substantial sill along the floor level of the bench ends: it served to keep in deep straw, which was there to keep worshippers' feet warm in cold weather!

Two more survivals are here too. At the east end of the north aisle is a rarity – an aumbrey complete with its original door and hinges. The aumbrey was a cupboard used in pre-Reformation times to store the holy oil and the sacred vessels and plate for the mass.

On the opposite side of the church, painted on the aisle wall, is a faded cross contained in a circle. This is a consecration cross, which takes us back to the very day on which this church was consecrated 650 years ago. The bishop would mark 12 crosses in holy oil, three on each of the walls, both inside and out. Later these would be painted over or carved. There are four carved ones at Alby, unusual examples carved in the backs of piscinas at South Creake and Holt, a very good painted one at Bale and others at Calthorpe, Lammas and Thrigby.

On the ends of the north aisle benches at Great Walsingham are carved images of the disciples, each with his particular symbol – symbols which, with the majority of saints in the calendar, indicate how they were martyred. The number of saints is legion. In Norfolk I've totted up 108 of them.

So at Walsingham one may make out St Andrew with his ×-cross, Thomas with a sword, St James the Less with a fuller's club (very distinctive – it looks like a hockey stick), Bartholomew with a flaying knife; and St John with a chalice. In the latter case the story is a different one – John was shipwrecked on an island where his 'hosts' thought to poison him… but the saint, divinely inspired, knew at once and made the sign of the cross over the cup given to him… and drank without harm. Therefore John is usually seen not merely with the chalice, but with a little devil or a snake curling up from it.

But let's move on to a church with some very unusual saints, each with a background story, at North Tuddenham, where the 15th century screen gives us Agnes, with dagger at neck and lamb at foot; Gregory, as a bishop, with crozier; Dorothy, with a spray of roses and a basket of fruit; Geron (or Jeron), robed as a priest and with a falcon on his gloved right hand; Catherine, crowned and with sword and her famous wheel; Etheldreda, crowned; Edmund, or possibly Sebastian, with arrow in right hand; and Roche, raising his robe to show the plague mark on his upper leg.

No space to tell all their legends here (but look them up in *The Popular Guide to Norfolk Churches* or in *The Oxford Dictionary of Saints*). But Barbara being a particular favourite of mine, I'll relate her tale in brief. Threatened with terrible torments in the early 4th century if she did not reject her Christianity, she refused – but looked forward rather to gathering flowers and fruit in her Saviour's garden. On the way to her execution, she was mocked by a young lawyer who jeeringly told her to send him some roses and apples. She was beheaded – but that night came in a dream to the lawyer… who woke to find the requested gift upon his pillow. He was converted – and followed Dorothy to martyrdom.

There are numerous screens in the diocese with equally intriguing saintly images. That at Ranworth is nationally, and justly famous. Litcham has a remarkable collection of saints, even though their images were brutally hacked in bygone, bigotted times. There's a beauty at Edingthorpe, where Bartholomew, Andrew and possibly Catherine are in evidence again, together with Paul (bible and sword), Peter (with his keys of heaven) and James the Great (with staff and scallop shell – wherein lies a very jolly tale). Above them the upper part of the screen is intricately carved, and is almost certainly 14th century in date.

But then, I'm hopelessly biassed when it comes to Edingthorpe – for me All Saints represents the perfect rural church, romantically sited on a rise with a view down to the north-Norfolk coast, picturesque outside with its round Saxo-Norman tower and thatched nave (don't miss the scratch dial on the porch) and enchanting and fascinating inside. Small wonder that, just after the Great War from whose pyschological scars he was still recovering, Seigfried Sassoon wrote about it lyrically.

Inside, white washed walls and ceiling, the colour of ancient wall paintings, venerable screen, endearingly battered 14th century chancel arch

Edingthorpe: St Christopher and the Christ-child look out from a mellow remnant of medieval wall painting

and homely furnishings combine with light and peacefulness into the perfection of the unspoiled English country church.

Among its wall paintings, which were discovered under plaster in the 1930s, is a super St Christopher, who provides an apt note on which to end this brief ramble through our priceless medieval heritage… to see him was to be sure of safety from harm that day. So he was usually painted on the north wall, immediately opposite the main south door.

Thus a traveller could open the door of the church (holding onto his mule with his other hand?), see the saint, cross himself with the holy water in the stoup beside the door – and go on his way contented. Which is what I invariably do after a day of happy church-crawling.

Photographs in this article are by Richard Tilbrook and are from his collection 'East Anglian Churches in their Landscape'

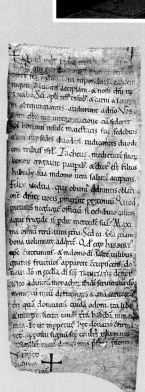

Top: *Dean Stephen Platten meets clergy in the cloisters following his installation.*
Above: *The cloisters form a magnificent covered walkway around the central garth.*
They were the link between cathedral and priory. Left: *The De Losinga Charter,*
dating from the early 12th century, granting land to Norwich Priory

When monks trod the cloisters

THE BENEDICTINE PRIORY AT NORWICH

JIM WILSON

STROLL in the monastic cloisters at Norwich and it takes little imagination to visualise cowled monks pacing these ancient walkways. For over four centuries the Benedictine priory dominated local life.

It was hugely influential. Its landed possessions matched those of a powerful Norman overlord. Twenty two manors in Norfolk and 87 churches paid revenues to the priory. Its manors and farms covered almost 2,000 acres. Tithes from its churches, and income from numerous smaller properties – mills, dovecotes, woodlands, marshes and houses – swelled its coffers.

In the thirteenth century the priory's annual income totalled £2,500, the equivalent of a substantial sum today. It drew funds from 150 parishes in the diocese, from Cockthorpe in the north to South Elmham in the south, from Wiggenhall in the west to Hemsby in the east.

In favourable years all profits went to the priory. If a manor made a loss the priory made good the deficit. So in hard times and poor seasons those who depended on the manors for their livelihood were guaranteed help.

Cells at Great Yarmouth, King's Lynn, Aldeby, North Elmham, Hoxne, and St Leonard's at Mousehold, were dependent daughter houses. Their activities were controlled by Norwich Priory and their Priors were selected from among the senior monks of Norwich.

The income of Yarmouth Priory was over £200 in 1355, although later it fell closer to half that amount. Its revenues included payments by fishermen of 'Christ's share' of their catch, equivalent to tithes on land. Lynn Priory had an income of £150 a year.

When Herbert de Losinga founded the cathedral and its priory, he brought to Norfolk a 60 strong community of Norman monks. From the beginning of the twelfth century to the second

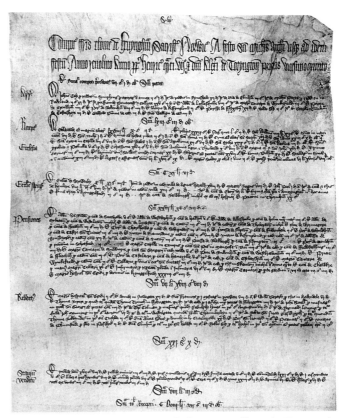

A portion of one of the 1,200 Obedientiars' rolls in the Dean and Chapter Records. This is the Sacrist's roll for the years 1405-6

half of the fourteenth the number of monks remained fairly constant. Then for another hundred years numbers dropped to 45, falling to around 35 when the Tudors came to power, and 18 at the Dissolution. But these figures account only for the monks. Scores of servants, skilled workers and craftsmen, were employed by the priory, so the total number living and working in proximity to the cathedral was closer to 250 at its peak.

The priory's purpose was to serve, maintain and equip the cathedral; to act as a charitable institution for the surrounding community, distributing to the needy; and to provide the care of a hospice. It fulfilled a role akin to a Middle Ages equivalent of the modern welfare state.

Its day to day business, during 270 years of its history, is chronicled in nearly 1,500 parchment rolls of the Obedientiars, the senior monks responsible to the Prior for running the institution.

Two thousand manor and account rolls have also survived giving a picture of the priory's influence in the diocese. Most of the Obedientiars' records, painstakingly written in Latin by paid scribes, are financial statements which kept the Prior briefed of his subordinates' progress in farming the priory's lands and conducting the business of the community. They answered the Prior's questions: 'Are we farming economically? Are we as a religious corporation operating within our means?' Together they are the best preserved day to day records of a medieval English monastery in existence.

The priory operated through twelve departments, each headed by a monk with executive authority. They were the Obedientiars. Chief among them was the Prior's 'major domo', the Master of the Cellar, or Master of the Prior's Chamber. He was responsible for entertaining the Prior's guests and managing the Prior's personal spending. He also supervised expenditure on major building schemes. His importance is emphasised by the fact that he controlled a staff of 50 stewards, clerks, squires and servants.

The Cellerar was responsible for feeding most of the occupants of the priory. His domain included the larders, where meat, fish and spices were stored, and the kitchens where huge quantities of

The lavatorium, an example of medieval plumbing where the monks made their ritual ablutions

food were prepared. By the standards of the time they lived well. The accounts record as many as 10,000 eggs consumed weekly and 230 loaves daily.

Two officials were solely responsible for the cathedral. Both offices survive today. The Sacrist, the only monk to sleep in the cathedral, cared for its fabric, furnishings, vestments, chapels and altars. His records mention the purchase of herbs and rushes to strew on the cathedral floor, oil for the altar lamps, and ten to twelve hundredweights of wax a year to make candles. In 1312, 1800 feet of rush matting were purchased for 13 shillings as floor covering in the cathedral. Half the Sacrist's annual income to pay for these items came from offertory boxes in the cathedral. The level of giving relative to income must have been high in the Middle Ages despite the poverty of most ordinary people. Collections made at the main altars and chapels in the cathedral averaged between £70 and £85 a year in the mid-fourteenth century.

The Precentor arranged the services, controlled the singers, cared for the cathedral's books and was responsible for the priory seal. Life must have been uncomfortable for the monks in the draughty, unheated cathedral in harsh winters. The Precentor's records show him providing large quantities of ginger to warm the brethren at worship and as an antidote to rheumatism, an occupational health risk in English monasteries.

Other Obedientiars included the Hostilar, who managed the priory guest hall, the link between the community and the outside world. From his inventory it is clear a number of rooms were attached to the Great Hall to accommodate visitors and priors of dependent houses. Their furnishings were lavish. Hangings decorated with birds and griffons, and beds with richly coloured curtains are mentioned. Visitors accommodated included reeves, bailiffs and tenants from the priory farms, and important guests of the Prior, their servants and clerks.

The Chamberlain was responsible for providing the monks with their clothing, shoes and bedding. He had a staff of 16 including four tailors who produced summer and winter tunics, robes and cassocks for the brethren. The priory must have been a good employer. One faithful servant, Thomas Tyngel, a tailor, is named frequently in the

Chamberlain's records over a period of 38 years. One wonders how his long service, stitching cassocks for the monks, may have been rewarded.

The Refectorer was concerned with the provision of meals for the monks, and the heating and lighting of their accommodation. The Almoner oversaw distribution of alms and food to the poor 'at the gates', and to prisoners, lepers and others under the priory's care. Almost 10,000 loaves were distributed annually to the poor together with charitable gifts of cloth and footwear. Some ten to eleven per cent of the priory's income went in charitable donations in kind.

The Infirmarer and his staff ministered to sick and elderly brethren. Purchases of sugar, almonds, cloves, mace, saffron, liquorice, and fennel indicate the kinds of herbal remedies used. The Gardener had charge of the priory's kitchen gardens, orchards and vineyard. Surplus produce was sold in markets outside the priory walls. Moles apparently were a constant problem to the Gardener and his staff. Payments to a mole catcher are recorded year after year. So are frequent expenses for implements – spades, forks, scythes and carts.

There was a strict heirarchy responsible to the Prior for administration of the priory's farms and manors. Most powerful was the Seneschal or Steward, the Prior's personal representative who had general responsibility for the whole of the priory estate. Next in seniority came the Obedientiar to whose department the revenues of a particular manor or group of manors passed. Finally, Sergeants, of whom there were a number, were responsible for the day to day supervision of workers at a particular manor or group of manors.

The Seneschal was clearly a man of considerable importance. In the thirteenth century he received an annual fee of £5, rising to £6 13s 4d during the fourteenth century. These were substantial salaries for the times. He was entitled to garments of coloured cloth and the best fur. He was closely associated with the Prior, often travelling the diocese with him on tours of the priory's lands. He also conducted manorial courts on behalf of the priory.

Woodlands were a source of considerable income. In 1273 Hindolveston Woods, the most valuable in the priory's ownership, provided a

The richly carved arch of the Prior's door dating from about 1310

revenue of £204 10s. Sheep farming was also a major source of income. The priory owned nearly 7,000 head of sheep towards the end of the thirteenth century. Sedgeford, the most profitable wool producing manor, contributed nearly £95 in 1265. The records tell of the priory acquiring more land expanding its manors over time, paying in the thirteenth century between eight pence and three shillings an acre, depending upon its fertility.

The institution's buildings covered most of what is now the Upper and Lower Close. The monastery lay to the south side of the cathedral, the Bishop's palace to the north, a deliberate separation between the wider political power of the Bishop and the business of the priory exercised by the Prior. Around this plan grew up responsibilities and duties which have their echo in the cathedral and the diocese today.

The most important buildings – guest hall, buttery, refectory, dormitory and Chapter House – were grouped around the cloisters. The role of the refectory in the life of the priory is emphasised by its size and architectural richness. 160 feet (48.76m) long, it had an arcaded wall passage around it approached by spiral staircases.

Set apart further to the south of the cloisters was the infirmary. Six columns of the infirmary hall, built between 1175 and 1190, remain on what is now a car park. The hall resembled a Norman church. To the east it opened into a chapel, so monks occupying beds in the infirmary hall could hear mass being sung. The infirmary was approached from the cloisters through the 'dark entry' and it was divided from the refectory by the infirmary garden, where medicinal herbs were grown. Elderly monks lived permanently in the infirmary with their sick brethren. Periodically, all the monks spent three days there after being bled a process regarded as the panacea for all ills. In some monasteries each monk was bled as frequently as every seven weeks.

The area now occupied by the cathedral shop, was the locutory, the room in which monks met and talked with travellers.

It is difficult to underestimate the importance of this powerful religious complex at the heart of the city. Monasteries were almost the only centres of education until Oxford and Cambridge were founded in the thirteenth century. They dispensed social aid and health care. Through their farms they contributed to the progress of agricultural science. They were substantial employers benefitting the economy of the region in which they were sited. They welcomed travellers at their guest houses and performed an indispensable service of shelter and safety when roads were poor, travel dangerous and a few miles the total distance one could expect to cover in a day. In the days before printing they were the only places where new books could be obtained by arranging to have existing manuscripts copied by hand. The work of such monastic institutions throughout Christendom lifted Europe from the Dark Ages to the relative enlightenment of medieval times.

The cloisters at Norwich form a magnificent 180 foot square walk around the central garth, and were the focus of priory life. They are the largest medieval monastic cloisters in England with the exception of the 13th century cloisters at Salisbury. Their function was to connect the various monastic buildings with each other and with the cathedral. Like so many other features of church architecture cloisters owe their origins to the warmer climate of southern Europe. In harsh winters they were less practical and it may have been to give the monks shelter in the draughty winter months that the east, south and west walkways have enclosed upper storeys, the only ones remaining in England.

The first cloisters were destroyed in the Tombland riot of 1272. Rebuilding commenced in 1297 and continued until completion in 1430. The slow progress is clearly marked in the traceries of the open window arcades. The Decorated designs of the first half of the fourteenth century reach a crescendo of flowing beauty and then stop abruptly. This point marks the arrival in 1349 of the Black Death which devastated the population of Norwich. Exeter, Winchester and Norwich were the worst affected dioceses in England as far as clergy deaths were concerned. There followed a 60 year pause before the work of rebuilding resumed. When it did, the new Perpendicular style had taken over.

Leaving the cathedral through the superb Prior's Door, which dates from about 1310 and was the main entrance to the monastic church through which the monks processed into service several times daily, one enters the east walk. To the left of the door canopied 14th century recesses are the remains of cupboards where the monks kept their books. The worn stones indicate where over the centuries monks stepped up to reach their books before entering the cathedral. On the lower of the two benches below the first recesses, scratched into the stonework, are hollows in the pattern of a popular medieval counters game, Nine Men's Morris. Shakespeare mentions the game in 'A Midsummer Night's Dream', but it was already old when Shakespeare was writing. Generally, conversation was forbidden in the cloisters.

Moving down the east walk from the Prior's Door one comes to a blocked entrance which led to the Slype, a passage into the end of the south transept with a room above used at one time as the Treasury and later as the Muniment Room. Next are triple arches, now filled by a wrought iron screen, which formed the entrance to the Chapter House, a building as large as the cathedral sanctuary and presbytery with a semi-circular apse at its east end. This was where the whole community met daily to discuss the business of the priory. The Benedictine rule demanded all important matters were to be considered by the brethren in council. This was where the Prior told his monks of demands upon their funds by the King, trouble in their churches, poor harvests, of visitors to the priory or of friction between city and priory. It was where erring monks were made to confess breaches of the Benedictine code and where they were disciplined. Further along the east walk is the entrance, also now blocked up, which led to the dormitory staircase, its step worn by the feet of generations of monks. The 'Warming' or 'Common House' was below the dormitory. In winter months a fire burnt there for the monks to warm themselves by. It was where they were allowed to converse, the forerunner of today's school or university common room.

Along the south of the cloisters as has already been mentioned was the great Refectorium or frater, the monk's dining hall, with kitchens at its west end. In the south west corner of the cloisters was the lavatorium, occupying two bays and dating from the fifteenth century. The pipes and taps which enabled monks to indulge in ritual ablutions have disappeared, but the stone trough which received the waste water remains. In medieval England monasteries boasted the most modern plumbing available. Further north along the west walkway is another doorway, which was the monk's entrance to the priory guest hall. Over it is a boss showing an open door, symbol of hospitality.

The Prior's Lodge, opposite the south east corner of the cloisters, is now the cathedral's Deanery. Except for brief periods during the Commonwealth and during part of the Second World War it has been the residence of the head of the cathedral for at least 700 years. The first building on the site was the Norman reredorter. The Norman buttresses of its east wall can still be seen either

side of the thirteenth century deanery front entrance. The north part of the deanery incorporates the majestic Prior's Hall, built about 1284.

Remains of other medieval monastic buildings can be detected in houses in the Close. The priory granary in the Lower Close was converted into dwelling houses at the time of the Dissolution and other nearby houses occupy sites of the brewery, bakery, stables, dove house and swannery. The priory was a major trader in local markets. Its records mention sales of hay, osiers, firewood, cows, calves, horses and milk.

In the Upper Close, beneath No 71 are the foundations of the Bell Tower, built originally by Bishop Eborard and re-built between 1299 and 1307 following its virtual demolition in the riot of 1272. Also in the Upper Close are flint faced buildings which were the offices of the Priory Cellarer and the Master of the Cellar. They are now converted into flats. The south west part of the Close, occupied by fine seventeenth and eighteenth century houses, was formerly the monastic Almonry, centre of the community's charitable work.

So what was life like for the monks who lived, worshipped and worked here? Their day was dominated by prayer. That was their main function and the rest of the priory's business from manual labour to study was fitted between the daily services in the cathedral.

The monks rose as early as 2.00 am and went straight from the dormitory to their places in the choir of the cathedral. The first services of the day continued, with short intervals, from 2.30 am until 7.00 am. The last of these was celebrated at daybreak. Between Prime and eight o'clock there was time for private prayer in the cathedral's side chapels. At eight the monks returned to the dormitory and the reredorter to wash and prepare for the of the rest of the day. Then they assembled in the cathedral again for Terce and Mass. At nine the whole community gathered in the Chapter House with the Prior. The rest of the morning was spent at various work – administration, reading, studying, copying and illuminating manuscripts and the like.

Soon after midday the community gathered to sing High Mass and at about 2.00 pm they adjourned to the Refectory for dinner – the main meal of the day. By this time they had been out of their beds for twelve hours without sustenance so it was a substantial meal. Beer was drunk with mead or wine on special feast days. Only one monk spoke at mealtimes. He was the brother deputed to read religious works as his fellow monks ate. The Benedictines believed in feeding the mind at the same time as feeding the body. The Prior had his own dining room where he entertained important visitors both male and female. An entry in the priory records for 1368 states: 'Wine at divers times for divers ladies in the Prior's chamber.'

Dinner over the monks went back to their labours in the cloisters and workshops. During these work periods some talking was allowed, but from the beginning of Vespers at 6.30 pm until after the Chapter meeting the following morning, ordinary conversation was strictly barred. If urgent communication had to take place or a visitor to the monastery needed to discuss something

These columns are all that remains of the priory's infirmary hall, the site of which is now the cathedral car park

the only place where conversation was allowed was in the locutory or parlour.

After Vespers the monks were served a drink and a simple snack in the Refectory before Compline, the final service of the day. Afterwards, at about 8.00 pm or slightly later in the summer, they went to bed, still clothed in their black habits. The Benedictine Rule laid down that each monk should have spiritual, intellectual and physical exercise every day. Their routine decreed they must participate in eight services in each 24 hour period and they were expected to sing through the whole of the psalter every month

It was not all work and prayer though. Roving players and minstrels visited the priory for feast days and often bands of players accompanied visiting nobility. The minstrels of the Earl of Suffolk, for instance, were at the priory regularly from 1366 to 1378. An entry in the accounts for 1328 says: 'Players, when the bailiff ate with the Prior, ten shillings'. Another for 1358 records: 'In wine and expenses among the singers at the Prior's feast, 6s 4d.'

Travel was an important, though often hazardous, feature of life. The Prior and his senior Obendientiars travelled extensively to the priory's manors and properties. Journeys to the ever-moving King's court, and to lay and ecclesiastical courts to settle disputes are frequently mentioned in the records. In 1272 the Cellarer travelled to Rome on priory business, possibly connected with the devastating riot of that year when the citizens destroyed many of the priory buildings and the city was punished with excommunication. The Sacrist undertook an epic journey to Rome during the years 1328 to 1330, incurring total costs of £167 10s, about the same as a short package tour in today's prices.

After nearly 420 years the Benedictine priory at Norwich was dissolved by order of Henry VIII in April 1538. The 34th Prior, William Castleton, became the first Dean of Norwich and the monks became canons or minor canons. A new phase of cathedral life began under Bishop, Dean and Chapter in the place of Bishop, Prior and cloistered monks. The new order of cathedral and diocesan life replaced the old, ensuring the continuity of both cathedral and diocese.

The Dean and Chapter library

TOM MOLLARD

NORWICH Cathedral has had a library almost since the cathedral's foundation. Herbert de Losinga was a scholar and collector. He wrote to the Abbot of Fécamp, the Norman Abbey where he himself studied and became Abbot, asking to borrow manuscripts for Norwich, and he set his young monks in the new Cathedral Priory to copying them. Before the invention of printing this was the only way works of scholarship could be reproduced. Herbert's letters handed down to us reveal a scholar who felt drawn, as many did in medieval times, towards secular literature as well as towards theology.

The book cupboards in the east and south walks of the cloisters indicate how books were stored for the use of the monks in the early days. The first collection of manuscripts was destroyed in the riot and fire of 1272, when the citizens burnt the cloisters. According to the Chronicler: 'everything the fire spared was plundered'.

The library was refounded, and grew in strength over the next 250 years, although we will never know how extensive the collection became, because no inventories have survived. However, records of the Priory after 1272 have been passed down. No other cathedral has so many rolls of the Obedientiars and manor and account rolls dating from the 13th and 14th centuries. Norwich's Dean and Chapter records are among the finest in the country and include some documents which do predate the 1272 riot. They relate to the foundation of the cathedral and its construction and maintenance, the defence of the monks' privileges, and the administration of the Priory and its estates. All are now in safe keeping in the Records Office.

The Dissolution in 1538 was the next blow to the library. According to the historian Blomefield: 'Return was made that there was no place convenient for it, and so all the members at that time pillaged it in a most shameful manner.' John Bale, writing soon after the event, said, 'I have been at Norwich, our second city of name, and there, all the library monuments are turned to the use of their grocers, candlemakers, soapsellers and other worldly occupiers.'

As a result of a commission's report, in 1570 the Bishop, John Parkhurst instructed the Dean and Chapter 'to repair and furnish their library within six months'. But by 1571, Leicester's man, Gardiner had become Dean, and one of his first acts was to demolish the library and dispose of its contents.

Nothing more is heard of the library for a hundred years, though at the Sequestration of 1643, when many church possessions and those of men opposed to the Parliamentary cause were appropriated, one of the library's most important surviving manuscripts, the 'Norwich Domesday', was nearly lost. It was saved, we are told, 'from the Turkish pawes of some of the lower rank of the heathenish Edomites, of whom Edmund Rust was ringleader.'

One of several works by Bishop Joseph Hall in the library, this one is dated 1671

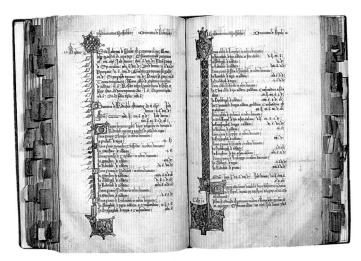

Ornamental border decoration on pages of the Norwich Domesday Book

The early fifteenth century Domesday Book of the diocese is a copy of an older one, and the beautiful writing is almost certainly that of one scholar.

Nothing else is recorded until 1673, when an upper room in the organist's house was reserved 'for use of this church as a Library'. In 1681 the Dean and Chapter ordered 'that a library be prepared for the reception of books to the use of the Dean and Prebendaries, and that the Dean contribute twenty pounds, and each prebendary ten pounds, either in books or money towards it, and that the Audit Chamber be the room set apart and prepared for that use'. From then on books accumulated steadily and under the care of Dean Prideaux the library was successfully re-formed.

It remained in the Audit Chamber until 1913 when Dean Beeching moved it to its present place above the south cloister. The library now contains some 8,000 volumes. Naturally it is strong in theology, particularly in its collection of 17th and 18th century pamphlets of which there are some 800 examples. Otherwise the subject matter is wide and varied, including history, law, philosophy, travel and topography, the early study of Anglo-Saxon and Runic poetry, and the natural sciences, besides the classical authors and the English poets.

It possesses some fine examples of the art of printing. Among the most significant is the Berner's Book, printed on the Caxton Press by Wynkyn de Worde, Caxton's foreman. The pictures of heraldry which it contains are some of the first known examples of colour printing. The library also has books which were the personal possessions of Edith Cavell.

The stock reflects the reading interests of the library's many benefactors who have left books to the library over the years. Dean Prideaux donated many volumes and other significant collections were left by Nicholas Penny (1745), Frank Sayers (1817), Dean Goulburn (1897) and Dean Beeching (1919).

In the 1880's, the library acquired the book-stock of the Norfolk and Norwich Clerical Society which had been founded in 1828. In the present collection about 6,500 books were printed prior to 1851. The stock is still regularly added to.

The library is a reference library and is available to the general public for that purpose. It is open for use every Wednesday.

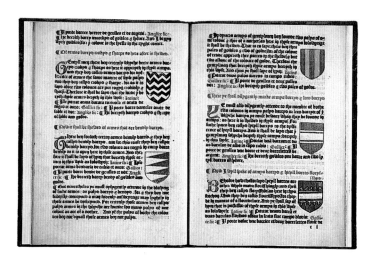

Berner's Book 1496, one of the first known examples of colour printing

Holy space to let people be

THE LIFE OF NORWICH CATHEDRAL TODAY

MICHAEL PERHAM *Canon Precentor of the Cathedral*

THERE are people who come to the cathedral and express surprise (even annoyance just occasionally) that services are being held; they thought they were coming to an historic monument in the hands of English Heritage or the National Trust. There are other people who come looking for the Bishop, imagining that he runs the cathedral or even spends the day on the welcome desk. There are yet others who only come for concerts and imagine it to be a cultural centre. Others, of course, have understood rather better, and know the place to be a 'working church', or the mother church of the diocese, or a place of sanctuary and refuge, or a centre of Christian learning. Few probably realise that it is all these things, and much more, and that that has its staff pulled in all sorts of directions trying to meet the needs of such a variety of visitors with their different expectations.

For the cathedral to fulfil its ministry it is vital that it should always have about it a sense of space, of peace and of holiness. If ever you have had the chance to be in it very early in the morning or late in the evening, when it is almost deserted, you can sense that very powerfully. But our task is to ensure that as much of that as possible is communicated to the visitor even in the middle of the day, even on a busy bank holiday, even when coming for a great service with a vast congregation. People need to experience that sense of space and peace and holiness. The extraordinary thing is that it takes a large staff, working long hours, and often apparently over busy, to achieve it.

What stops those who work those long hours from losing their own sense of the peace and holiness of the cathedral is the priority we give to worship. The casual visitor who is surprised by the fact that there is a service going on could not be more wrong! Worship really is at the heart of cathedral life, and we put enormous resources

The installation of Dean Platten in September 1995

into it. It isn't simply the conventional thing to say that worship is what it is all about. We really do believe that and work to make it so.

I find it helpful to identify five categories of service, or, more accurately, categories of people for whom we provide services. Their needs are all rather different.

An historic event – the first ordination service for women priests in April 1994

Photo: E.C.N. Ltd

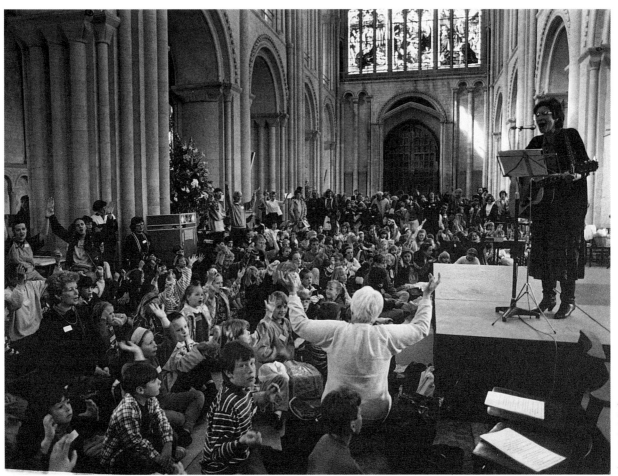

Five hundred children join in a Diocesan Children's Festival

Photo: E.C.N. Ltd

The first is the 'foundation'. This means, in effect, the clergy, the choir and the vergers, who meet each day for worship, and who are joined by a small group of other lay people who would almost qualify for honorary membership of the foundation. We are, in a way, the successors of the Benedictine monks. We occupy the same stalls, we sing the daily services as they did, and we do it, whether there is any other 'congregation' or not, because it is a vital part of our community life. Every day begins with Morning Prayer and with the Eucharist in a different chapel each morning. Every day ends with Evening Prayer, most of the time sung as 'Evensong' with music from across the Christian centuries. Visitors sometimes join us and people hovering in the nave or transepts overhear us, but essentially this is a religious community saying its prayers.

But then there is the second category, the 'cathedral congregation'. This is a larger group of two or three hundred people who worship in the cathedral at the Sunday Eucharist and on other festival days. They can't be there every day, for they are getting on with their life and Christian witness in the world, but the cathedral has become for them the equivalent of a parish church. It can't be quite like that, for it is differently governed, and its congregational life is only part of its broader mission. Nevertheless the people who form its congregation are very important to it, and their worship needs have to be met. That demands a subtly different style from that of the foundation.

Thirdly there is the diocese, and the cathedral as the setting for major diocesan liturgies. The cathedral is 'the bishop's church', not in the sense that he runs it from day to day, but because his 'cathedra' (throne or, better, teaching chair) is in the cathedral. When he wants to bring all his clergy and people together, the natural place is the cathedral, which therefore becomes the setting for ordinations, for the inauguration of new ministries, for visitations, children's festivals, an annual reader's service, and much more. These great acts of worship, often involving more than a thousand worshippers, have to reflect yet another style, bringing together creatively the tradition of cathedral worship and the regular experience of worship in the parishes, so that people go away

uplifted and encouraged. People, rightly expect the cathedral to set high standards in liturgy as in much else.

There are also, fourthly, occasions when the cathedral plays host to county, civic and community occasions, and services for many organisations, from the Scouts to Age Concern, as well as to services for Remembrance Day, Battle of Britain Sunday and the like. Each of these is different, though most have in common that quite a large number of those who come are not regular churchgoers, and their visit to the cathedral is perhaps their only experience of Christian worship.

Finally there is the worship that the casual visitor, who comes for some quite other reason, encounters and is sometimes drawn into. There are prayers said on the hour through the middle part of the day and there are celebrations of the eucharist at the altar under the tower. The visitor can join in, or, as is often the case, half join in, staying on the edge and participating in a way that doesn't demand too much. We never know how much good is done that way, but we suspect that people's lives are often touched by that sort of encounter, coming upon Christian worship almost unawares.

These five categories of worship may mean that, in an average week, there will be nearly thirty services to be maintained. Some of them need only a little preparation (though they all need some). Others, like the daily choral Evensong, require planning and rehearsal. Some, like a Memorial Service, a Confirmation or a Carol Service, may involve many hours of work by many people. All those people work to one of the two full time cathedral canons, the precentor, and answerable to him is a large department of workers, paid and voluntary.

First among these is the cathedral choir, more immediately under the leadership of the Organist and Master of the Music, who is assisted by the Assistant Organist and an Organ Scholar. The choir consists of twelve men, six of them 'lay clerks', paid a small salary by the cathedral but also holding down '9 to 5' jobs in the city, and six of them 'choral scholars' studying (usually music) at the University of East Anglia. There are up to twenty choristers, aged between 7 and 14, and all

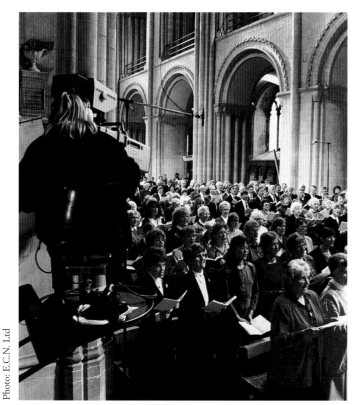

Ancient and modern – a high-tec camera records 'Songs of Praise' for national television

'All God's creatures' – Gillian Shephard then Minister of Agriculture, and former Dean Paul Burbridge at a farming festival, 1993

of these are educated at Norwich School (which is not quite a choir school, for the Dean & Chapter are not the governing body, but the relationship with the school is a close one). A Choir Endowment Fund, managed independently of the Dean and Chapter, by a group of trustees pays a bursary towards the education of all choristers, and would increase the scale of that bursary if an increase in the capital in the fund allowed. It is a demanding life in the choir, with services six days a week and practices nearly every day. The boys start singing at 8.20 in the morning and their school day goes on until the end of Evensong at about 6 pm, and then there is homework to do. It is a good life, but it requires commitment and a professionalism that most boys of that age are not asked to show.

At the time of writing the cathedral is launching a new girls voluntary choir, not tied to one school and not involving daily services, but with some cathedral services as well as opportunities to sing around the diocese. Giving girls a chance to share the cathedral singing experience is part of a trend to equal opportunities that is now marking many aspects of cathedral life that used to be male preserves.

Among these other areas are the Guild of Stewards, who welcome people to worship and help with the smooth-running of large services (especially the ones where the precentor requires a congregation of several hundred to move around the cathedral!), and the Guild of Servers, who are also involved in regular and special services, carrying cross and candles and sharing in all the symbolic and ritual movements of the liturgy that add beauty and colour to every occasion. The servers are an area where young people may make a real contribution to worship.

Services also require much work of the office staff – a seemingly endless stream of special service sheets to be drawn up and sufficient copies made, and sometimes tickets sent out. And the Sacrist's staff, the vergers, are also involved, moving furniture, putting up stages, bringing in chairs. It always seems as if no two services have the same requirement.

Mention of the Sacrist and his staff moves us on to the other major area of cathedral life, the welcome to visitors. Again this is a large department answerable to the other full time canon, the Canon Pastor. Every day to some extent, and at a higher level from Easter to the autumn, there is an army of people, mainly volunteers, at work in the cathedral to ensure that anyone who comes in receives just the right welcome, information and help. It's a subtle business, for some are looking for a lot of help, some others simply to be allowed to wander undisturbed. There are people on the Welcome desk, guides, chaplains, shop staff, buffet staff, and more. There are tours, school parties, and special trails. The place is often milling with people, but somehow it must go on being a holy place, with a sense of space and peace. That is difficult to achieve sometimes, but everybody involved knows it is the aim. Senior among those who assist the Canon Pastor is the Visitors' Officer, often on the telephone making arrangements for tours and pilgrimages and school visits, or encouraging the volunteers on the desk, and sometimes acting as the cathedral's press officer too. This side of the cathedral's work suffers from inadequate premises – shop, buffet, schools project work all need better and bigger space and can hardly cope with the increase in the tourist industry and the interest in heritage. A new Visitors' Centre is a high priority for the cathedral now.

But it is the Sacrist's office that is often the first port of call for the visitor, especially the one who has come with a specific purpose. Situated right in the middle of the church, under the pulpitum and between nave and choir, it is the nerve centre of the cathedral through the day. The Sacrist is, in effect, the cathedral floor manager. Like his staff of sub-sacrist and five vergers, you may sometimes see him dressed up and carrying a silver wand (verge) in a procession, but more likely erecting staging, answering extraordinary questions from those arriving at his office door, or doing an emergency repair to a leaking roof.

Of course a proportion of those who come to the cathedral come with specific and real needs. Some are "down and out" and in need of food and always wondering whether they might be given money (they rarely are). Some are distressed; some crisis has overtaken them and they

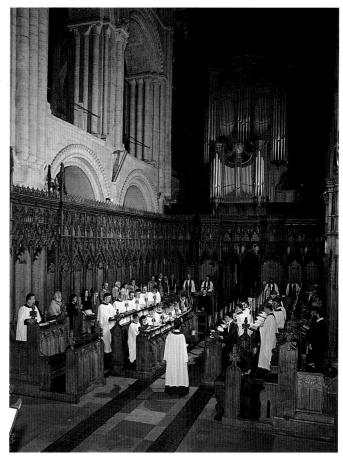

Continuity – the choir occupies the carved stalls originally used in monastic times by the Prior and monks

need to talk to somebody. Some simply need a corner in which to think or cry or pray. Perhaps the cathedral is the right place to which to come because there is something anonymous about it; people can seek help here and go away unrecognised. Almost anybody on the staff may find themselves helping those who come with a special need, but there is the particular ministry of the Pastoral Assistant, on loan to us from the Community of All Hallows at Ditchingham. In a variety of ways we try always to be ready to offer the ministries of listening, counselling, spiritual direction and healing. Sometimes we fail, but it isn't through lack of trying.

It may be only half true to speak of the Sacrist's office as the nerve centre of the cathedral. For hidden from the view of the visitor across the Close at No 12 are the Cathedral Offices. You cannot run an organisation as big as this without good administrative back up. The Administrator and Chapter Clerk, a layman, heads the administration and is treated as a member of the Dean and Chapter, the "board of management" in effect of the cathedral. With him work the Accounts Manager and several secretaries, who labour to keep the show on the road, and answer the telephone to people with questions about almost every aspect of Norfolk life and religion. Quite why they ask us the times of services in the Methodist Church in Lowestoft or what Quakers believe about the Holy Spirit, heaven only knows, but they do, and we try to find the answer. No 12 is also the home of the Friends of Norwich Cathedral, who do sterling work in encouraging volunteer support for the cathedral and in raising large sums to maintain the fabric.

Within the offices is the Chapter Room. Here various meetings are held – the Senior Staff Meeting (clergy and senior lay members of the paid staff), the Cathedral Community Committee (members of the congregation), the Fabric Advisory Committee (expert advisers on the cathedral building and its conservation), and the Dean and Chapter. The Dean & Chapter which is the governing body of the cathedral, and which meets twice a month, consists of the Dean, three Canons Residentiary – the Precentor, the Canon Pastor and the Librarian (who is also the Archdeacon of Norwich) – two Honorary Canons, representing the diocese and bringing the insights of those outside the immediate cathedral community, and the Administrator. As the leader of the cathedral team, the Dean is the chairman. His role is to hold the community together, like the abbot in earlier times, to develop relationships with the county, the city and the diocese, to represent the cathedral in the wider community, and, inevitable in today's world, to be something of an entrepreneur and a managing director, and still to be holy!

The Dean & Chapter are also well served by their expert advisers – the Surveyor, the Steward of the Close, the Archaeologist, and others. For they are responsible for a historic monument (the cathedral is that even if it is much else) and for a host of listed buildings in the Close. Careful stewardship of its resources are called for, lest, like some other cathedrals, the Dean & Chapter make a foolish decision in relation to buildings, finance or the treasures of the cathedral.

Another important building in the Close, part of the cathedral's mission, is the Christian Study-centre, which shares a building, Emmaus House, with the Training Team of the diocese. Here under the auspices of the cathedral, courses are held for lay people to study and discuss aspects of the Christian faith and its relationship to other disciplines. For cathedrals have traditionally been places of learning, and this tradition is still alive. Deans and canons find less time than in the past to write books, though some do manage it still, and scholarly sermons are out of fashion (though in the cathedral people are always wanting copies of sermons so that they can study them at home). But the Study centre is one of the contemporary ways in which the cathedral goes on being a place of learning. There is a need for further developments in this area, as in the related area of evangelism, where cathedrals have sometimes been unduly coy and hesitant.

The are other failures too. The difficulty is that cathedrals today are presented with so many opportunities to serve people and to tell the good news of Christ, and our problem is finding the time and the resources to do new things, and to do them well. When were fail it may sometimes be through lack of vision, but more often it is simply that we are too stretched.

But we should never be dispirited, for the truth is that cathedrals do not rely on human efficiency or initiative to make their impact (though both can help). The building speaks for itself of history, of beauty and of God, and the building provides a holy space to let people be. Norwich Cathedral is wonderful without us, but it is a rare privilege for those who work here to co-operate in making it more wonderful still.

Edith Cavell, Norfolk heroine

PHILLIP McFADYEN

THE Reverend Frederick Cavell came to the Norfolk village of Swardeston soon after he was ordained. He evidently knew what he was taking on as he had spent some years as the curate of neighbouring East Carleton. He liked Swardeston so much that he remained there for the rest of his ministry, some 46 years. Frederick Cavell was trained for the ministry at King's College, London and his certificate is to be found hanging at the back of Swardeston church. While he was training in London, he fell in love with his housekeeper's daughter, but they were not to be married until she had completed some extra education and was thought fitted to the role of a parson's wife. In 1863, after twelve years at East Carleton, Frederick Cavell accepted the living at Swardeston. Two years later, Edith Louisa Cavell was born.

At first the Cavells lived in a temporary parsonage some distance from the church on the edge of Swardeston's beautiful common. This fine Georgian farmhouse is still standing and known locally as 'Cavell House' as it was here that Edith was born in 1865. In that same year, a new Vicarage was built next to the Church.

This was the house in which Edith grew up and knew as her home. It was here that the three younger children, Florence, Lilian and John, were born. The Vicarage was built at Frederick Cavell's own expense and local people say that it nearly ruined him. He was always a 'poor parson' from that time. Even if the family were poor and the food not very appetising, they were concerned to share what they had with their poorer parishioners. Sunday lunch was a great family affair and whatever was cut from the Sunday joint, an equal amount was taken out to the hungry cottagers nearby.

Sundays in a Victorian Vicarage could be gloomy by today's standards. No cards, or books allowed except the Bible. Frederick Cavell was something of a Puritan and would want to keep a strict Sabbath. Edith wrote to her favourite cousin, Eddie, 'Do come and stay again soon, but not for a weekend. Father's sermons are so long and dull'. It is said that the Cavell children did occasionally sneak a game of cards in the study when Father was in church. They certainly were not the dour and sour Victorians that biographies suggest. The Vicar would easily be tempted to disguise himself as a bear and cause the Cavell children to shriek with delight.

Childhood

When Edith was a girl, she was aware that her father badly needed a church room to house the growing Sunday School for the children of the village. She determined to do something about it. She wrote to the Bishop of Norwich, John Thomas Pelham, a grand but kindly man whose impressive tomb can be seen in the north transept of the cathedral. She told him of the problem and he agreed to help, provided the village would raise some of the cash. Within a short time, Edith and her sister were making good use of their artistic talents and had painted cards which they sold to help raise some £300 for the church room. Edith wrote to the Bishop reminding him of his promise and so the church room was built adjoining the Vicarage. To all accounts, it was very well used. Both Mrs Cavell and Edith taught in the Sunday School and acted as godmothers to a number of local babies, who in later years still treasure their signed copies of the Bible and *Pilgrim's Progress*. Sadly, this church room was sold by the diocese at the time of the sale of the Vicarage. The church always has a fine show of flowers and the Cavell Festival weekend nearest to the date of her execution (12th October) has become an annual Flower Festival, when the village give thanks for Edith's memory and invite people to share in her appreciation of God's creation.

Edith could never have known she was to become a heroine and martyr but she is said to have confided in a lighthearted way to a friend that she would like to be buried in Westminster Abbey. The first part of her impressive funeral took place there, attended by Queen Alexandra, Princess Victoria and many others from all walks of life with military and nursing representatives from many parts of the world. By popular demand, her body was brought back to her native Norfolk and lies in Life's Green in the Cathedral Close. The grave is well tended and nearly always covered in flowers. Among Edith's most treasured possessions were the roses sent by her nurses, which she kept in her cell long after they were spent, as a comfort and a reminder of the roses at the Vicarage in Swardeston.

Schooling and first jobs

Edith and her two younger sisters, Florence and Lilian, had their early education not at the recently opened village school but at home. Later in 1881, Edith is thought to have spent a few months at Norwich High School, when it was housed at the Assembly House in Theatre Street, Norwich. From sixteen to nineteen years old, Edith went to three boarding schools; Kensington (possible St Margaret's, Bushey – a school for poor clergy families), Clevedon, near Bristol, where she was confirmed (15th March 1884), and finally Laurel Court, Peterborough, in the cathedral precincts, where she learned to become a pupil teacher. There were many such establishments at this time, unashamedly providing what was boasted as a 'high moral training'. Laurel Court was fairly typical, ruled by a 'fearsome dragon' and the place smelt of 'cats, margarine and treacle' (according to one ex-pupil). However, French was well taught here, with ten minute conversation as part of the daily curriculum. Edith showed a flair for it and as a result was recommended for a post in Brussels in 1890. Prior to this she took several jobs as a governess. Her first job was to look after a clergy household in Steeple Bumpstead. Despite the demands of her

job, she still found time to keep up her hobbies of tennis and dancing. She once danced till her feet bled, which ruined her new shoes but cured her chilblains! She is remembered as being full of fun, always smiling and wonderfully kind to the children in her charge. She was, for a short time, governess to some of the Gurney children at Keswick New Hall in the next village and was affectionately remembered. At about this time, Edith was left a small legacy and decided to spend it on a Continental holiday. She spent some weeks in Austria and Bavaria, and was deeply impressed with a free hospital run by a Dr Wolfenberg. She endowed the hospital with some of her legacy and returned with a growing interest in nursing.

Edith in Brussels

In 1890, Edith took a post with the Francois family in Brussels. She stayed there for five years and became a firm favourite with the family, even though she objected to their jokes about Queen Victoria being a prude. She continued to paint in her spare time and became fluent in French. Her summer breaks were spent in Swardeston, playing tennis and painting. A romantic attachment with her second cousin Eddie emerged at this time. Edith might have accepted him had he proposed but he confided to another cousin that he felt that due to an inherited nervous condition, he perhaps ought not to marry. They appear to have been in love and Edith never forgot him, for she wrote on the fly leaf of her 'Imitation of Christ' 'With love to E. D. Cavell' on the day of her execution.

Nursing as a career

1895 saw Edith's return to Swardeston to nurse her father through a brief illness. He remained vicar until his retirement in 1909. Helping to restore her father to health made Edith resolve to take up nursing as a career. After testing her vocation for a few months at the Fountains Fever Hospital, Tooting, Edith, at the age of thirty, was accepted for training at the London Hospital under Eva Luckes in April 1896. In the summer of 1897, an epidemic of typhoid fever broke out in Maidstone. Six of Miss Luckes nurses were seconded to help, including Edith. Of 1700 who

Photo: E.C.N. Ltd

Edith Cavell

contracted the disease, only 132 died. Edith received the Maidstone medal for her work here – the only medal she was ever to receive from her country. Edith did not impress the redoubtable Miss Luckes, who was to say of her that 'Edith Louisa Cavell had plenty of capacity for her work, when she chose to exert herself' ... and that 'she was not at all punctual'. By today's standards, the hours were demanding (7am - 9pm, with half an hour for lunch) and the pay miserly (£10 a year).

Edith was recommended for private nursing in 1898 and dealt with cases of pleurisy, pneumonia, typhoid and a Bishop's appendicitis. She soon moved back into the front line of nursing and in 1899 was a Night Superintendent at St Pancras, a Poor Law Institution for destitutes where about one person in four would die of a chronic condition. At Shoreditch Infirmary, where she became Assistant Matron in 1903, she pioneered follow up work by visiting patients after their discharge. Those early pastoral visits with her mother in Swardeston obviously had a lasting effect.

Back to Brussels

In 1907 after a short break, Edith returned to Brussels to nurse a child of Dr Antoine Depage but he soon transferred her to more important work. Dr Depage wanted to pioneer the training of nurses in Belgium along the lines of Florence Nightingale. Up until then, nuns had been responsible for the care of the sick and however kind and well intentioned, they had no training for the work. Edith Cavell, then in her early forties, was put in charge of a pioneer training school for nurses, 'L'Ecole d'Infirmiere Dimplonier' on the outskirts of Brussels. It was formed out of four adjoining houses and opened on October 10th, 1907.

Edith rose to the responsibility immediately; despite her own early record of unpunctuality, she kept a watch before her at breakfast and any unfortunate woman more than two minutes late would forfeit two hours of her spare time. The work was quickly established, despite some resistance from the middle classes. Edith writes home ... 'The old idea that it is a disgrace for women to work is still held in Belgium and women of good birth and education still think they lose caste by earning their own living.'

However, when the Queen of the Belgians broke her arm and sent to the school for a trained nurse, suddenly the status of the school was assured. By 1912, Edith was providing nurses for three hospitals, 24 communal schools and 13 Kindergartens. In 1914 she was giving four lectures a week to doctors and nurses alike and finding time to care for her morphia addict niece and a runaway girl, as well as her two dogs, Don and Jack.

War declared

Edith often returned to Norfolk to visit her mother, who since her husband's death was living at College Road, Norwich. They also had holidays together on the North Norfolk coast. She was weeding her mother's garden when she heard the news of the German invasion of Belgium. She would not be persuaded to stay in England. 'At a time like this', she said 'I am more needed than ever'. By August 3rd 1914, she was back in Brussels dispatching the Dutch and German nurses home and impressing on the others that their first duty was to care for the wounded irrespective of nationality. The clinic became a Red Cross Hospital, German soldiers receiving the same attention as Belgian. When Brussels fell, the Germans commandeered the Royal Palace for their own wounded and 60 English nurses were sent home. Edith Cavell and her chief assistant, Miss Wilkins remained.

The initial German advance was successful. The British retreated from Mons and the French were driven back, many in both armies being cut off. In the Autumn of 1914, two stranded British soldiers found their way to Nurse Cavell's training school and were sheltered for two weeks. Others followed, all of them spirited away to neutral territory in Holland. One, from the 1st Battalion of the Norfolk Regiment, recognised a print of Norwich Cathedral on the wall of her office. She was always delighted to receive someone from her beloved Norfolk, asking a private Arthur Wood to take home her Bible and a letter for her Mother. Quickly an 'underground' lifeline was established, masterminded by the Prince and Princess de Croy at a chateau at Mons. Guides were organised by Phillippe Baucq, an architect, and some 200 allied soldiers were helped to escape. (The password was 'Yorc' – Croy backwards). This organisation lasted for almost a year, despite the risks. All those involved knew they could be shot for harbouring allied soldiers.

Edith also faced a moral dilemma. As a 'protected' member of the Red Cross, she should have remained aloof. But like Dietrich Bonhoeffer in the next war, she was prepared to sacrifice her conscience for the sake of her fellow men. To her, the protection, the concealment and the smuggling away of hunted men was as humanitarian an act as the tending of the sick and wounded.

Edith was prepared to face what she understood to be the just consequences. By August 1915 a Belgian 'collaborator' had passed through Edith's hands. The school was searched and while a soldier slipped out through the back garden, Nurse Cavell remained calm. No incriminating papers were ever found (her diary she sewed up in a cushion). Edith was too thorough, and she had even managed to keep her 'underground' activities from her nurses so as not to incriminate them.

Two members of the escape route team were arrested on July 31st, 1915. Five days later, Nurse Cavell was interned. During her interrogation she was told that the other prisoners had confessed. In her naiveté she believed them and revealed everything. Many people think that Edith 'shopped' her compatriots simply because, like George Washington, she could 'never tell a lie'. This was far too simplistic an explanation. Edith was willing to abuse her position in the Red Cross to help her fellow countrymen in need. She would have equally protected her colleagues at the risk of compromising her own conscience, even though this would have been painful and contrary to her upbringing. She was trained to protect life, even at the risk of her own. 'Had I not helped', she said, 'they would have been shot'. The explanation is that Edith simply trusted her captors, was glad to make a clean breast of it, and willingly condemned herself by freely admitting at her trial that she had 'successfully conducted allied soldiers to the enemy of the German people'. Herein lay her 'guilt', and this was a capital offence under the German penal code. She was guilty, so they must shoot her.

Nurse Cavell's last days

The German military authorities, having sentenced Edith and four others to death, were determined to carry out the executions immediately. Despite the intervention of neutral American and Spanish embassies, Miss Cavell and Phillippe Baucq were ordered to be shot the day after the trial, October 12th, at the National Rifle Range (The Tir Nationale). A German Lutheran prison chaplain obtained permission for the English Chaplain, Stirling Gahan, to visit her on the night before she died. His account of her last hours is very moving. They repeated the words 'Abide with me' and Edith received the Sacrament. She said:

> *'I am thankful to have had these ten weeks of quiet to get ready. Now I have had them and have been kindly treated here. I expected my sentence and I believe it was just ... Standing as I do in view of God and Eternity, I realise that patriotism is not enough, I must have no hatred or bitterness towards anyone'.*

Edith was magnanimous in her death, forgiving her executioners, even willing to admit the justice of their sentence. This sentence was carried out hurriedly and furtively in the early hours of October 12th. Two firing squads, each of eight men, fired at their victims from six paces. Stories were told that the men fired wide of Edith, that she fainted and was finally dispatched by a German officer with a pistol. Reliable witnesses report nothing of this and it seems the executions were carried out without incident. However there has recently come to light a collection of press cuttings dating from 1919 to 1974 compiled by a J. F. Randerson of Canterbury. This devotee of Edith's memory records what he calls a 'strange confirmation' of Arthur Mee's story that one of the firing squad refused to take part in the execution. Private Rimmel is said to have thrown down his rifle when ordered to fire at Nurse Cavell and to have been shot by a German officer for refusing to obey orders. A near neighbour of Randerson testified to being present at a secret exhumation of a German soldier who had been hastily buried near the grave of Edith. There may be some truth in the story that the firing squad were reticent and that one of them may have been shot with the brave British nurse.

The outcry that followed must have astounded the Germans and made them realise they had committed a serious blunder. The execution was used as propaganda by the allies, who acclaimed Nurse Cavell as a martyr and those responsible for her execution as murdering monsters. Sad to think that this was contrary to her last wishes. She did not want to be remembered as a martyr or a heroine but simply as 'a nurse who tried to do her duty'. The shooting of this brave nurse was not forgotten or forgiven and was used to sway neutral opinion against Germany and eventually helped to bring the USA into the war. Propaganda about her death caused recruiting to double for eight weeks after her death was announced.

Edith's return to Norfolk

Edith had been hurriedly buried at the rifle range where she was shot and a plain wooden cross put over her grave. You can see the shaft of this cross preserved at the back of Swardeston church. When the war was over, arrangements were made for Edith's reburial. At first, Westminster Abbey

was considered but the family preferred Norfolk. Her remains were escorted with great ceremony to Dover and from there to Westminster Abbey for the first part of the burial service on May 15th, 1919. A special train took the remains to Norwich Thorpe Station and from there, a great procession moved slowly to the cathedral. Bishop Pollock described her as 'alive in God' and as someone who taught us that our patriotism must be examined in the light of something higher. She was laid to rest outside the cathedral in a spot called Life's Green. Here services are held annually on the Saturday nearest the anniversary of her death.

Her character continues to fascinate us today. Anna Neagle made a film of her and Joan Plowright appeared in a very successful play called 'Cavell'. Sadly there was a time when her name was associated with an extreme form of patriotism, despite her words that this is 'not enough'. As a result, some have shied from her memory. A truer assessment of her should be to recognise her as she saw herself – simply 'a nurse who tried to do her duty'. Her perception of duty challenges us today; in achieving the greater good (or the lesser evil), we may need to compromise our reputation and even endanger our good name. Edith, in doing what she considered her duty, was prepared to go further and surrender her life and liberty to relieve suffering and help others achieve freedom.

What are Friends for?

ELSPETH MACKINLAY

WHEREVER you look in Norwich Cathedral – upwards at the great roof, outwards at the Norman stonework or inwards at the precious artefacts that enhance our worship, the Friends of Norwich Cathedral have probably made their present superb condition possible. Since the association's formation in 1930, with the aim, in the words of Dean Cranage, 'to help and support the Dean and Chapter in all discharge of their obligations to maintain and embellish the fabric and furnishing of the Cathedral Church in the spirit which inspired its founder, Herbert de Losinga, when he caused its building to be undertaken', the Friends, now 3,500 in number, have raised and spent hundreds of thousands of pounds over the years to make this possible.

A modest start in 1930, boosted by support and donations from the King and Queen and other members of the Royal family and a minimum subscription of five shillings for members (reduced in 1935 to two shillings and sixpence for clergymen!), has led to today's continuing and loyal partnership between the cathedral and the thousands of individuals and groups, including whole parishes, companies and organisations, who have rallied round, like good friends, over the last 66 years with money, gifts, special skills, time and devotion.

The Friends have been further inspired by the leadership of two remarkable High Stewards: Sir Edmund Bacon from 1956 to 1979 and Earl Ferrers from 1979 to today. There is a beautiful window in the Jesus Chapel dedicated to Sir Edmund, but in reality his true memorial is the restoration work completed in the 60's and the 70's on the tower, roof and spire. It was his own view that had this been left undone, the spire would not have withstood the great gale of January 1976. Earl Ferrers, who succeeded him, is also a Norfolk landowner and, in addition, a Government minister. In spite of many London

and county commitments, his tall and imposing presence has been highly visible in the Sunday morning congregation for many years.

Norwich is the only cathedral in England and Wales whose Friends have been solely responsible for the upkeep of the fabric and have managed steadily to find finance, even in times of great national hardship. Decisions are taken in association with the Dean and Chapter by the Friends' Council, a group of laymen and clergy

Earl Ferrers, High Steward of Norwich Cathedral

Photo: E.C.N. Ltd

drawn from members of the association. Currently, and for the first time, *English Heritage* are contributing to the massive project involving the refurbishment of the tower, spire and the great west window and costing some £900,000.

The box of annual reports in the Secretary's office at 12, The Close have a good tale to tell, mirroring the vicissitudes of the years. An early priority was the designing of a membership badge, silver (ten shillings) or bronze (three shillings). Armed with this, Friends did not have to pay the small levy at the time to tour the east end of the cathedral. In fairness, when charges were abolished in 1948, the Friends agreed to meet any shortfall from admission funds and establish collection boxes and captions.

Chunky reports with learned articles on the cloister bosses in the late 30's gave way for years to thin utility versions with many articles held over for better days – which never appeared. Nothing prepared members for the shock of tax and post-war price hikes. In 1933, 30 new chairs gifted in thankfulness for a loved one safely home after the Great War cost one pound two shillings and sixpence each. Chairs bought by the Friends in 1981 were £50 each. The years reflect the cost of weather and storm damage, air raid precautions and bomb damage, new fire prevention measures in 1985 and 1986 after the York Minster tragedy, outrage over the imposition of VAT on repairs, the effects of a growing tourism market and the increasing involvement of laymen in cathedral life.

Publicity has often been by personal approach like 'Operation Snowball' started in 1968 and many of the early traditions still remain and are thoroughly enjoyed today. There are a series of winter lectures in the Prior's Hall and in addition to a New Friends Evening in the autumn, there are two annual special events, Friends Day in the summer and the Wine and Cheese party in the winter.

Members enjoy a couple of outings a year to other places of special interest – soon after the formation of the Ladies Committee in November 1938, plans were afoot for the very first summer outing to Peterborough. Sadly it was not until 1947 that the habit was resumed when 96 Friends enjoyed a day in Cambridge. (Tea two shillings and sixpence, coach seven shillings and sixpence,organised by Mrs Blofeld of Hoveton).

The Ladies Committee, now the Publications Committee, have put in decades of devoted work. From 1948, their steady sale of Christmas cards climbed from 3,000 to 22,000 in 1952 and 93,000 in 1994. Every day from May to November, the Friends run a table in the nave with the current selection. The cathedral has always been graced by beautiful flower arrangements and linen – in 1946, Mrs Brown led a team of Friends who repaired and restored the cloth and vestments when no coupons were available for replacements.

As with the Ladies Committee, some of the same family names have echoed down the decades and gifts have poured in with a generosity of spirit reflected in the love of the cathedral by the people of Norfolk and Norwich. Ninety oak trees were donated in the early 70's from local estates for the aisle roofs. Valuable carpets, crosses, candlesticks, pictures – many from anonymous donors, have boosted funds. On many an occasion, a generous legacy has made all the difference to work in progress. After the devastating organ fire in 1938, the next few reports document the ups and downs of paying the bills, finally settled in1950 when the Friends not only managed £2,000 for the new organ case but £421 for the acoustic system and £100 for new choir robes.

When the spire was overhauled in the early 1960's, the Friends paid £11,800 towards the total cost of £32,800, defrayed further by a gift of £50,000 plus the enrolment of 400 new Friends in a single year allowing plans for the new north and south nave roofs to go ahead without delay. A magnificent fundraising event, an Antique Fair run by the Friends, many of whom sacrificed personal heirlooms, raised £30,000 and work was completed in 1975. Countless gifts, plus the resources of the Friends then, now and in the years in between, have made the present rolling programme of maintenance possible to keep the 900 year old building safe and secure for the next millennium.

SIGNIFICANT DATES
IN THE HISTORY OF THE CATHEDRAL AND DIOCESE

1091	*Herbert de Losinga appointed Bishop of Thetford*
1094	*Seat of Bishopric moved from Thetford to Norwich*
1096	*Herbert de Losinga lays foundation stone of Cathedral and founds the Benedictine Priory*
1101	*Dedication of Cathedral*
1119	*Death of Herbert de Losinga: buried before High Altar*
1121-45	*Completion of Cathedral to west door by Bishop Eborard de Montgomery*
1171	*Nave damaged by fire*
1194	*Norwich granted City Charter by Richard I*
1245-57	*Bishop Walter de Suffield builds Lady Chapel*
1272	*Tombland Riot: Priory, Cloisters and Cathedral severely damaged*
1278	*Cathedral consecrated in presence of Edward I*
1297	*Rebuilding of cloisters commenced*
1325	*Ethelbert Gate completed*
1362	*Spire blown down in hurricane: damage to presbytery and clerestory*
1381	*Bishop Henry Despenser defeats Peasants Revolt*
1420	*Erpingham Gate erected*
1463	*Spire struck by lightning: nave roof destroyed*
1472	*Bishop Lyhart completes stone vault over nave*
1480	*Presbytery vault and spire built by Bishop Goldwell*
1509	*Transept roofs destroyed by fire. Bishop Nykke starts building of transept vaults*
1538	*Dissolution of Benedictine Priory: New Foundation of Dean and Chapter*
1549	*Kett's Rebellion*
1578	*Queen Elizabeth I visits Cathedral.*
1643	*Puritans pillage Cathedral: Civil War disturbances*
1650	*Petition from Gt Yarmouth to use lead and materials from the Cathedral to build a workhouse and repair piers*
1830-90	*Extensive restoration by Anthony Salvin and Sir A.W. Blomefield*
1847	*Re-discovery of Despenser reredos*
1914	*Diocese of St Edmundsbury and Ipswich formed reducing size of Norwich Diocese*
1919	*Edith Cavell buried at Life's Green.*
1930	*St Saviour's Chapel built on site of medieval Lady Chapel. Formation of Friends of Norwich Cathedral*
1942	*War damage to transept roofs*
1952	*Extensive restoration commenced*
1958	*Royal Norfolk Regimental Chapel dedicated*
1959	*Ancient throne restored*
1964-5	*Renovation of spire and tower*
1968	*Bauchon Chapel restored as Chapel of Friends of Norwich Cathedral*
1966-70	*Rebuilding of nave outer roof*
1988	*Restoration of St Catherine's Chapel*
1994-5	*Renovation of tower and west window*

CATHEDRAL DIMENSIONS

Length	**140.5** *m* (461 *ft*)	*Height of nave vault*	**21** *m* (69 *ft*)
Breadth	**22** *m* (72 *ft*)	*Height of presbytery vault*	**26** *m* (85 *ft*)
Length of transept	**54.25** *m* (178 *ft*)	*Height of spire*	**96** *m* (315 *ft*)